CONCILIUM

concilium 1991/1

THE BIBLE AND ITS READERS

Edited by

Wim Beuken, Sean Freyne
and Anton Weiler

SCM Press · London
Trinity Press International · Philadelphia

February 1991

ISBN: 0 334 03006 4
ISSN 0010–5236

Typeset at The Spartan Press Ltd, Lymington, Hants
Printed by Dotesios Printers Ltd, Trowbridge, Wilts

Concilium: Published February, April, June, August, October, December.

For the best and promptest service, new subscribers should apply as follows:
   US and Canadian subscribers:
Trinity Press International, 3725 Chestnut Street, Philadelphia PA 19104
Fax: 215–387–8805
   UK and other subscribers:
SCM Press, 26–30 Tottenham Road, London N1 4BZ
Fax: 071–249 3776

Existing subscribers should direct any queries about their subscriptions as above.

Subscription rates are as follows:
United States and Canada: US$59.95
United Kingdom, Europe, the rest of the world (surface): £34.95
Airmail to countries outside Europe: £44.95

Further copies of this issue and copies of most back issues of *Concilium* are available at US$12.95 (US and Canada)/£6.95 rest of the world.

Contents

Editorial

The law books of Moses (Deut. 31.24–26) and Ezra (Neh. 8), the scrolls of Isaiah (Isa. 8.16–17) and Jeremiah (Jer. 36) and the book of secret revelations of Daniel (Dan. 7.1; 12.4) are vivid reminders that God's word was always associated with a book that had to be read in and to a community of faith. They are also concrete images of the possibilities and difficulties of current understanding of the written word, which always requires an interpretative framework. The early Christians were heirs to this tradition of the written word also (Luke 1.1–4), but they were equally conscious of the distance between text and reader and therefore of the need for interpretation (II Peter 3.15). The rise of printing brought about enormous changes in terms of text production (translations!) and reading practices, but these changes only accented the need for biblical interpretation in the life of the church. Modern biblical criticism may be seen as the continuation of this hermeneutical enterprise, despite the development of new methodologies, which were the direct result of the Enlightenment and its concerns.

Today, biblical scholarship is undergoing a shift in methodological emphasis towards an appreciation of the texts themselves as literary productions in reaction to the dominant scholarly preoccupation with the historical events behind the texts. This also involves a greater awareness of the role of the reader in the art of interpretation. This new emphasis draws considerably on contemporary theories about the nature of literary texts and their reception and some would query the appropriateness of these theories for understanding biblical texts, based as they are on current philosophical and literary fashions. This issue of *Concilium* seeks to map the change of emphasis in biblical scholarship generally, while exploring its possibilities and limitations for reading the Bible as scripture in the church.

Section One deals with the contemporary problem of the plurality of reading experiences of biblical texts in two different ways. B. F. Meyer discusses the methodical challenge to a single sense of scripture – the presupposition of the historical-critical method – that arises from modern literary theories about texts and readers. A. van der Heide addresses the same issue by considering the different ways in which a single passage of scripture has been and is interpreted differently by Jews and Christians.

In Section Two the ways in which the Bible has been read within the faithful communities of two thousand years are documented in five articles, focussing on certain milestones of the historical process. C. Kannengiesser describes the emergence of the Christian way of reading the Bible and of the Christian canon in the early centuries. G. Stemberger gives a survey of the history of the Jewish use of the scriptures. P. Valkenberg explains the mediaeval monastic and scholastic way of reading the Bible, as related to the cultural circumstances, the appearance of the Mendicants and late mediaeval popular preaching. C. Augustijn discusses the fundamental change of interest arising with the Reformation. The Bible read and explained becomes the very heart of Protestant spirituality and cult. J.-R. Armogathe does the same with regard to the Enlightenment. The very fact that text criticism expanded enormously during the eighteenth century brought new incentives for the long-standing question of the composite sense of scripture. Thus, the historical perspective of this section highlights the key interpretative factors that have always been at work both in terms of the texts and their readers.

In Section Three, inevitably, the question arises as to how the Bible is being read today. In three articles the contemporary situation is critically evaluated in the light of the declaration of Vatican II regarding the Bible in the life of the church. C. E. Gudorf makes us see that the official uses of scripture by the *magisterium* show a great variety of approaches, from the employment of special task-forces of exegetes by the USA bishops to the Roman appeal to scripture, which is often still of the proof-text variety. Next, S. McEvenue addresses the question whether in fact the aspiration of Vatican II, which called for scripture to become the soul of the church, has been realized in liturgy and preaching. Finally, C. Mesters points out that the central role of scripture reading in the struggle for liberation in Latin America offers a very different contemporary paradigm, which is paralleled by the hermeneutical models of other traditionally marginalized groups.

In a concluding article in Section Four, D. Tracy reflects on the historical and contemporary phenomenon of the variety of Bible reading. He offers a theoretical evaluation of how it is both possible and necessary to integrate modern critical approaches, especially literary ones, within an ecclesial perspective, if the Bible is to continue to function as a critical challenge to our assumptions (Isa. 55.10; Heb. 4.12).

Wim Beuken
Sean Freyne
Anton Weiler

The Congress: An Appraisal

Jean-Pierre Jossua

Several months after the second *Concilium* Congress, held at Louvain in September 1990, it is at least possible to attempt a short appraisal. This is certainly a partial evaluation, since it is dependent on a single point of view, that of its author.

The preparations for this congress went through several successive stages, during which its scope was widened. To begin with, the plan was to bring together about a hundred theologians to discuss a specific subject, with no concern for wider communication; then the number was increased and a broader theme was chosen; finally it was decided to allow three hundred 'observers' (students, interested persons) in addition to the invited 'members', and to welcome the press. This development, which sought openness, inevitably went wrong: the discrimination between two categories of participants, who were not allowed to have an equal say, was resented as being an unfair privilege, all the more so since a number of theologians in the strictest sense had been enrolled as 'observers' once the quota of two hundred 'members' had been reached. Tensions could certainly be felt at the Brussels Congress in 1970, but the seven hundred observers had not protested.

Be this as it may, on the first full day steps were taken to prevent the meeting being poisoned by the problem, and all distinctions were abandoned. However, the result of this was that the 'theological congress' became a *forum*, for better or (almost) worse, above all during the general assemblies in the afternoons. To the degree that there was some success in directing the course of these assemblies somewhat towards the theme of the day, those participants who wanted to make interventions outside any planned theme felt the procedure repressive.

It will be remembered that to put ourselves 'on the threshold of the third millennium', each of these three days, devoted respectively to memory, to the present and to anticipation (though these moments of time could be separated), had been prepared for by a special issue of *Concilium* published at the beginning of the year. On the first evening, after speeches by the President, Anton van den Boogaard, and Cardinal Danneels, they were to be complemented by a paper linking the congress to the Second Vatican Council. Edward Schillebeeckx had been invited to give it, but could not do so for health reasons; remarkably, it was improvised at a few days' notice by Giuseppe Alberigo.

In the general sessions during the morning, once the authors of the preliminary papers had spent a few minutes summarizing them and bringing them up to date, younger challengers, who were not directors of the journal, attempted a critical analysis and a complementary contribution. Exchanges in the study groups, which were arranged according to language, were to allow discussion of all these propositions – a discussion which was generally calm and fruitful, and which was much appreciated – and prepare for the general assemblies in the afternoons. The enormous amount of material which formed the ingredients of these different interventions could be classified under five distinct headings: 1. lists of grievances about the church's past; 2. reasons for anxiety about the present state of the church and society; 3. theological foundations for a constructive attitude towards the challenges of the present and the future; 4. major tasks for today; 5. signs of hope offered by observation of and participation in present-day movements in church and society. It would not be particularly interesting to list all this material here, and impossible to synthesize it.

However, to imagine from what has just been said that the Louvain Congress was an intellectual event would be to have a wrong idea of it. It was somewhat disappointing in this respect, whether because of the performances themselves or because of the difficulties in carrying out a rather complicated task. Above all, though, the Congress was an extraordinary scene of *encounter*. Theologians, men and women, from fifty-one countries, introduced themselves to one another, listened and made friends. Many isolated people were able to have their fill of conversations, and felt strengthened in points of view which at home were sometimes minority, even a cause for persecution. Numerous other meetings took place on the fringe of the congress and thanks to it: women, Spanish-speaking theologians (many regretted that this had not been an official language), Québécois, Dominicans, and so on. The cafés of old Louvain, helped by the clement weather, played a by no means negligible role in this dynamic of first meetings or reunions. In this respect the climate was really very different from that at Brussels in 1970: more humour, no obsession with producing 'motions' of which ultimately no one took much notice, more stardom of the 'great' theologians, who were listened to respectfully, a stress on the discussion groups. But to stop at the level of encounter as such would not be to get to the heart of things.

In fact the great difference from the previous congress was neither at the level of friendship nor, at the other extreme, at that of content. It has to do with the *new voices* which made themselves heard in the planned interventions, the groups and the assembly: those of lay people, of women, of Africa, of Latin America and of Asia, and of Christians from Eastern Europe. This was not talk about them, but their own voices, the voices of men and women. These were different and even discordant voices, sometimes provocative or incantatory, and at all events difficult to integrate into the 'masculine-clerical-university-Western' theological discourse which still predominated in the preliminary contributions or the 'challenges'. At the end of the congress it was said on several occasions that a theology of witness had been juxtaposed with a discursive theology. But again we need to make this rather more specific.

It is true that on the platform the two kinds of intervention seemed irreconcilable. All one could do was listen in a brotherly or sisterly way. But on the one hand these 'different' theologians had themselves also produced formally argued works or articles which others read and of which they often take account. And on the other hand there is a whole 'Western' theology which distrusts the reign of the concept and is based on witness. The decisive point here is that the question is not primarily one of 'witness' (of faith) but of 'narrative' (of situation). Social reality – the reality of discrimination; extreme destitution; political, cultural or religious oppression – constantly crops up as the unavoidable context of Christian existence and reflection. That is what changes many things, and it is perhaps not so much a strictly theological problem, whether one likes it or not, as a political and ecclesial one. We shall return to that later. I end this section by pointing out that we did not hear many young voices – although the average age was not very high – and that the presence of some friends from the East did not disguise the fact that the cards have not yet been redealt in Europe, despite the tremendous changes that have taken place in the last two years.

To return to the more worked-out theological contributions that we read or heard at this congress. It is of some interest to try to discover their style and method. First of all we recognized a *militant* and even resolutely ideological discourse in which a current struggle, with its tools of analysis, serves as a criterion for the interpretation of the New Testament and the history of Christianity. Its power of renewal was noted on several occasions, but so was the peril of seeing it set up as a sole key, and the risk of arbitrariness in historical reconstructions. Then there was a *critical* discourse bearing on church practices and representations. There was agreement as to the value of this, but note was also made of its contextual and relative character over against other contexts of the life of the church in the world. Then there was an *apologetic* discourse: an unresolved question of human existence, not to mention a terrible problem of present-day life on the planet, was raised and a response was given from the gospel. This is certainly an acceptable way of arousing motivation to action – as was the case here – but such a suggestion becomes very dangerous when one goes on, as often in the Catholic church, to the content of self-styled 'Christian solutions'. However, there were fears at Louvain that the analysis itself, in its radical pessimism, was not sufficiently influenced by a concern to set salvation in Christ over against the depths of our impoverishment. Then there was a *meta-theoretical* and typological discourse, vigorously illuminating our intellectual situation, with a risk of abstraction and detachment from cultural experience, which is always so complex. Finally, in the text from Gustavo Gutierrez – who was absent because he was occupied in urgent humanitarian tasks in his country – and in the interventions by his friends, there was a *confessing* discourse in which the negative and militant pole of the discussions opened up a space in which to hear the essentials of the biblical message. I should say in passing that Jon Sobrino was given a standing ovation by the congress in place of and on behalf of the absent and those who have disappeared.

Having started on this small topic in a way which must necessarily remain incomplete, I note with a kind of retrospective stupor the disappearance of both the *deductive* discourse and the *historico-positivistic* discourse which forty years ago still constituted the entire production of our discipline and in renewed forms was still dominant at Brussels in 1970. In all the cases here a lever external to the theological field – a cultural and factual lever – has been at work. And this discovery can lead us to grasp one of the reasons for the contrast – and the difficult relations – between this collection of theologies, diverse though they are, and what is officially approved in the Catholic church and indeed forms the basis for teaching delivered with authority: we might call it 'neo-Roman', but labels are never satisfactory.

In this connection it is important to note that the Congress was marked by a remarkable absence of polemic against the 'official' theology of the church. There were certainly references to doctrinal positions – sometimes institutional, sometimes ethical – improperly imposed by the authorities since there is reason to think them historically relative; or unjustly to accuse theologians of causing present ills when in fact they have limited their effects; or again the favouritism often shown to theology which justifies and legitimates, not to mention a kind of sworn-in theological officialdom. But these were only passing remarks. The proceedings which some people began here against an oppressive or improperly masculine Western Christianity was aimed as much at 'open' Western theology as at the official theology, and moreover it sometimes seemed so sweeping that one could ask what in the current of Christianity continued to attract this or that platform.

This moderation of intra-ecclesial theological criticism is certainly the reason for the relative failure of a very vigorous draft resolution which some friends put to the vote of the assembly: it challenged some statements in the text on the vocation of the theologian published by the Congregation for the Doctrine of Faith, but it also took a stand on various moral or institutional problems. It was approved by more than two-thirds of those present on the last morning, but it did not attain the three-quarters majority required for it to become a declaration of the Congress. Several people privately explained their abstention on the grounds that they felt that the text did not fit in with what actually took place.

I should add here that another motion had been planned by a group of feminist theologians. Since it arrived too late – according to the procedure announced at the beginning – it could not be put to the vote. Addressed to the directors of *Concilium*, it was aimed at increasing the involvement of feminist theologians in the various sections. A certain number of women present at Louvain felt some unease: does not feminist theology have a tendency to set itself up as the sole expression of the voice of women? Does *Concilium* need more women or more feminists? This question is very relevant from the perspective of several Western European countries.

It is certainly quite easy to denounce in other ways of doing theology than ours, institutionally more integrated, or in certain styles of pastoral government, a discord between the gospel proclaimed by the church and what is in fact practised. This discord can become hopeless distortion when domination is justified by service, obedience by freedom, or riches (collective) by poverty (individual). But on several occasions at Louvain people had the courage to raise more disturbing questions. An authentic charity, the sincerest and most disinterested zeal for the truth, a passion for unity, can have perverse effects: it can conceal the demands of justice, a lack of respect for the conscience, a simplistic approach which obliterates the most fruitful differences. The best intentioned, not to mention the most competent, recourse to scripture can allow the most varied interpretations and sometimes the most terrifying justifications. As an antidote, we were reminded of the absolute necessity not to telescope the lowliest, the most common human intermediaries: reason, scrupulous truthfulness, the demands of justice, and respect for the freedom and physical persons of others. No religious legitimation for suspension of these basic attitudes should be allowed. And though some friends were able to speak – vigorously, and not without their reasons – of what has been the reverse of our 'modernity' in formerly 'colonized' countries, we should forcibly remind ourselves that we owe to this modernity some of the basic requirements in the very name of which we at present question it.

As to criteria for theological activity, at Louvain, thanks to some of the papers and forum discussions, we were able to see quite a precise sequence which was perhaps the most consistent theoretical contribution of the meeting. Its starting point was the idea of *memory* as a basis for Christian reflection and practice. But it appeared that if memory can prove subversive, more often it tends to become perhaps repetitive and an expression of identity. It proves fruitful only if it is questioned by an evocative, acute *present* – one of positive, new experiences or of suffering and struggle –, for it is by bringing these two poles together that 'history' is made fruitful, both as a discipline of the knowledge of the past and as something which it is the task of humanity to construct. Here too there can be a rebound: if the criteria for a contemporary struggle can prove a decisive stimulus to the birth of a new memory of Christianity, it can also prove a heavily ideological and univocal factor, subjecting memory to an intolerable reduction. That will happen unless, in turn, memory accepts questioning by a third authority, that of the *Word*: this same text, which from one side we scrutinize in the light of our present perspectives and questions, turns back and affects us in its irreducible otherness: through it, 'God' speaks. Can we stop there? Do we not know that the authority of the Word has been both the basis for witness to the Infinite which shatters our self-sufficiency and our limited horizons and the discourse which legitimates sacerdotal power: a transcendence situated behind us is always ambiguous. So we need another criterion, that of *imagination*, which innovates while relying on earlier authorities, and which for the believer is ultimately focussed on an expected transcendence. We shall come back to this.

On the way I noted several reasons for uncertainty, along with a reticence in the face of peremptory reaffirmation of supposed evidence. It is striking to note that during the congress these inevitable uncertainties were taken into account without any sign of fear or those hollow extravagances which usually indicate flight in advance, and that there was a stress on the need for general consent to an ongoing quest and a recognition of being on the way. A reassuring representation of 'postmodernity' was rejected with a demonstration that there could be no going back on the critical vigour of thought, but rather that there had to be a 'Nietzschean' radicalization of this latter. Theologians were humiliated by being reminded of their incompetence to interpret their time beyond a modest discernment of 'signs of the presence of Christ' or convergences with the gospel message. And it was not even the major weakness of our meeting – which was very evident to me – not to be able to interpret itself in these terms. In fact when we announced that we were going to put ourselves on the threshold of the third millennium, we showed virtually no capacity for anticipation of the future of Christianity, whether in the form of analysis or scenarios: we did not leave the area of our ideas and our presesnt experiences. But did we not say that we are on the threshold of something that we do not know how to name; that we cannot divide the future into periods; that the illusion of a radical change to come would be as fatal as that of an unproblematical continuity? Is not the absence of security for the future itself a decisive stimulus to going forward? Could the lack of a utopia which might mobilize the church and theology be the sign of a discretion and modesty which is more reassuring in the face of the unforeseeable than any disturbing features in our lack of creativity?

Clearly the orientation of a utopian dream depends on an analysis of the present. The majority of the speakers, while not sharing the reassuring illusions of a 'basically Christian Europe' or those who promise a return to religion through the 'new evangelizations' of the media, seemed ready to refer to an ambient religiosity. They did so perhaps to take into account a secret desire for God which only needs encouragement, or to denounce a false religion which can only blur the free and constructive encounter of men and women with the God of Jesus Christ. At all events, the exchanges revealed that for many other theologians, above all the Europeans, the essential problem to face is that of an explicit or practical unbelief, of an indifference and an ignorance about the basis of the Christian message: the choices of the gospel, the figure of Jesus, the nearness of God. This unbelief and indifference are certainly no longer aggressive, but they keep growing, and have reached the point of becoming a real tidal wave among those under twenty-five. Some traditional strongholds, or at the opposite extreme some happy personal discoveries, make no difference to this massive phenomenon, which affects all spheres and is inseparable from the upheavals in lifestyles which also affect the other components of culture.

Beyond indicating an impasse in the communication of the faith, do not these facts confront theology with the question whether Christianity will continue to be capable of offering a symbolic point of reference by which men and women can give meaning to their existence, cope with their major problems, and achieve social integration? To appeal to the most decisive human spiritual experiences falls short of ensuring that the question of God will be raised, far less that the gospel will be accepted, along with the risk of faith to which it issues a call, commensurate with the risk taken by God in history and humanity. Demonstrating the limits of the criticisms of religion and working for the intellectual credibility of the faith falls short of being confronted with the fundamental factors of this change characteristic of the end of our second millennium: Christianity in the West is tending to become the religion of some individuals and some communities, committed indeed, but in the last resort insignificant. There is nothing to indicate that the so-called 'postmodern' development is going to change anything here. Many indications suggest that economic development in Eastern Europe – as clearly as the swing of the pendulum after the religious persecutions where they took place – will have (and in the Third World would have) very much the same effects as those which secularization had on the social reality of Christianity in the West, leaving aside individual destinies.

Such was the fruit of some of our conversations at Louvain. The fact remains that the massive questions forced on us were those from the southern part of our planet: those of the poorest who are getting still poorer, those of the voiceless, those of people frustrated by their own culture. In this connection the evening devoted to a round-table discussion on the situation of theology in the different parts of the world was particularly impressive. I could call it an economic and political problem. It is also a major ecclesial problem, since it is entirely the churches which, under the cover of being apolitical, keep playing *ad infinitum* the game of the oppressive oligarchies and their omnipotent external allies. It is also a theological problem, if we leave aside the aggressive and rather puerile questions about past responsibilities and ask about how much weight our way of doing theology today should carry in these debates and struggles.

In this respect a degree of unanimity seemed to emerge. On the other hand, attentive though people proved to be to the threats weighing on the future of life on earth, a certain difference in evaluations appeared: from absolute catastrophism to a still-confident vigilance over methods of forecasting and a growing will to remedy current degradations or to prevent the worst catastrophes, via some intermediary positions. For the most pessimistic, hope is an out-of-date and illusory theme which must be replaced by responsibility. But would this responsibility be possible without hope, and is not a certain ideology of hope which used to be fashionable involved here?

That is why in the end it seems to me that a combination of three elements is necessary for a positive vision of the future to be offered us. First of all there is a demanding and competent sense of responsibililty, based on analyses which are both precise and wide-ranging, which do not always coincide with a generous adherence to the revolutionary developments of the nineteenth century. Then there is the discreet but penetrating voice, often heard at Louvain, which tells us that we can learn hope from those men and women who have suffered and continue to hope in limited horizons, with minimal success and repeated failure, under the threat of immeasurable and uncontrollable forces. And finally there is the creative imagination of which I spoke above and without which no new hypothesis will arise. The great historian Paul Veyne, in his splendid book on René Char, explains the involvement of a poet in the Resistance after the occupation of France. This involvement was rare, undertaken only by some men and women who were open to the unknown, perhaps in a completely non-religious way; 'The situation seemed desperate in 1951: but Beauty, which is good, does not teach only what one should do; it also suggests that one can do it and that imagination knows this longer than reality.' Does God not have the slightest power of suggestion? Are the theologians deafer than the poets?

Around 1972 a first phase in the history of *Concilium* seemed to have been completed: that devoted to the attempt to universalize the theology of the Second Vatican Council along the lines of an open and constructive reception. The directors of the journal were then able to start on a new period, marked by openness to the human sciences and to interdisciplinary studies, and soon by finding a place for Third World and feminist theology. We might suppose that the Louvain congress has been the fruit of this. Now a new decade should begin with a broad renewal of perspectives, for to represent 'His Majesty's loyal opposition' is not sufficient orientation for theological research, even at a time of authoritarian pressure and crisis. Will we be able to say one day that this same congress was also the starting point for that?

Translated by John Bowden

I · The Contemporary Situation

The Challenges of Text and Reader to the Historical-Critical Method

Ben F. Meyer

Historical-critical method and reader-response theory

The term 'historical-critical method' has now been in use for approximately 200 years. Over this period its connotations have been relatively stable: philologically learned, critical (as opposed to 'dogmatic'), and devoted to scientific (as opposed to 'pre-critical') interpretation and history. For the first two-thirds of this 200-year period, 'historical-critical' work was largely aligned with the tradition of interpretation and history set in motion by Benedict Spinoza (1632–1677).[1] Its main virtue was resolute commitment to philological and historical evidence; its main vice, a certain discord with the biblical tradition itself, an alienation of sorts that pervaded the critical distance of interpreter or historian from the biblical text.

In the nineteenth century, doctrinally conservative Protestants were suspicious of the devices of historical-critical scholarship, and began to adopt them only very gradually and cautiously. Catholics were especially slow to draw on the full range of historical-critical resources; Catholic scholars collectively and Catholic exegetical scholarship became a force to reckon with only in the wake of the Encyclical Letter *Divino Afflante Spiritu* (1942). A principal result of the conservative Protestant and Catholic contribution, however, was to alter the anti-doctrinal connotations of the term 'historical-critical' and to subvert the supposition that historical-critical work proceeded on the basis of *one* method grounded in a single (scientistic or positivist) philosophy.

An anti-dogmatic current, equipped with congruous philosophic resources, has persisted in biblical scholarship through the end of the nineteenth century to the present, earning the name 'radical criticism'.

Although undiscriminating religious critics continued to blame 'the historical-critical method' for the experimental results of 'radical critics', more discerning observers distinguished philological and historical methods from the defective philosophic assumptions that were often tacitly and gratuitously fused with them.

Indeed, philosophic assumptions underlying the practice of literary and historical criticism have gradually, though not universally, won recognition as exercising remote but significant control over results. Hermeneutical suppositions, in other words, lurk behind or hover over criticism and condition its operations – even when the hermeneutical suppositions are quite unthematic. This is an often overlooked factor in the rise to prominence, since the late 1960s, of 'reader-response' criticism.

The latter is among the most recent in a series of literary-critical movements that have vied for the space once occupied in literary criticism by 'formalism' and in biblical criticism by positivism. The positivist notion of objectivity has never been entirely overcome among practitioners of historical-critical methods. Wherever science makes its appearance, it is immediately dogged by scientism, as by a shadow. (Scientism is misinterpreted science and naïve philosophy.) Nevertheless, over the past few generations scientistic or positivist objectivity has lost the *dominant* position it had in the nineteenth and early twentieth centuries. The mid-twentieth century witnessed a Neo-Kantian and existentialist repudiation of positivism. Bultmann ridiculed and discredited the notion that commitment to truth called for the suppression of subjectivity.[2] But the Bultmann acknowledgment of subjectivity proved to be a halfway house. True, it tempered the objectivism fused with 'historical-critical' methods by promoting an existentialist, decision-oriented anthropology. But it did not articulate a coherent account of knowledge, and by the 1960s its theological programme had run out of steam. The initiative in biblical scholarship passed from theology to social-scientific studies (which we shall leave out of consideration here) and to literary criticism.

In Europe and North America, literary criticism in the mid-twentieth century was dominated by formalism (focus on the inner perfection of the text, the paradigm being the lyric poem) and 'close reading' (especially attention to how the parts or facets of the text related organically to one another and to the whole). In the United States the New Critics concentrated all attention on 'the poem itself', repudiating (under the rubric 'the intentional fallacy') attention to its causes,[3] and (under the rubric 'the affective fallacy') attention to its effects.[4] In 1967 E. D. Hirsch, Jr challenged the repudiation of interest in 'intention'[5] and in 1971 Wayne C. Booth, in the first of a series of studies of rhetoric, challenged the repudiation of interest in 'effects'.[6]

In its beginnings, however, reader-response criticism did not contest the hermeneutical centrality of the text; for these beginnings were constituted by the discovery and thematization of 'the implied author' (that voice in which the text of poem or novel or essay spoke) and of the correlative 'implied reader' (the reader implicitly called for and addressed by the implied author). The voice of the text and its distinct tone, which varied in accord with illocutionary modalities (arguing, promising, threatening, etc.) and perlocutionary modalities (the intending of effects: to move to shame, to instil pride, to provoke reflection, etc.).[7]

In time, however, both European and North American theorists, having more thoroughly explored the many dimensions of the act of reading, began to entertain such theoretical options as dispensing, first, with the 'author', then with 'the text'.

The author was abandoned as soon as 'the intended sense' ceased to be acknowledged as the object of interpretation. The text was abandoned or, more exactly, lost its primacy, as soon as the reader was recognized as indispensable to its construction. These two proved to be the pivotal developments in reader-response (or reader-reception) theory, over the past twenty years. As such, they do indeed pose a 'challenge' to interpretation as hitherto practised. The challenge might be epitomized in the claim of the 'reader' to have become king. 'Meaning' was now taken to be the product, not of the textual realization of an author's intention, but of a reader's 'realization' of a text otherwise mute. No longer a stable artefact, the text yielded centre-stage to the reader's creative cognitive activity.

Before we take up the issue of challenge to the historical-critical method, however, we are obliged to step back and survey the hermeneutical resources that allow us to distinguish authentic and inauthentic elements in both the practice of historical-critical methods and in the movement of reader-response criticism.

Critical realist hermeneutical reflections

There is a realism, grounded in sense knowledge, that from childhood on is natural to the human subject. The infant acquires a sense of the real by seeing, hearing, touching, tasting and smelling it. As the child grows and develops, to be sure, it moves haltingly through the world of the senses into the larger world of the story, and with time begins to qualify its original sense of the real by learning to operate on more complex bases. The moment at which this momentous adaptation and transition takes place is referred to traditionally as 'the age of reason'. It is entry into the world mediated by meaning, and by progressively more varied and layered meaning. The child's experience at home and at school fosters the laborious entry into this ever larger, more engaging world.

In the world of sense, or of immediacy, an object is what is seen, heard, tasted, smelt, felt. In the world mediated by meaning, on the other hand, an object is what is wondered about, what is specified by questioning, understood when the question is relevantly answered, and known when the answer is secured as true.

Corresponding to these two senses of 'object', there are two senses of objectivity. The condition of the objectivity of sense-knowing is the proper functioning of the senses. But the condition of objectivity in the world mediated by meaning is complex. An experimential component lies in the givenness of data. An intelligent component lies in the demand for intelligibility, which is expressed by a question and met by a relevant answer. Finally, a rational component lies in the further demand that the answer be true, met by the assembling of evidence and the reflective grasp of it as 'sufficient'.[8]

The root of this intelligent and rational procedure is at once a common experience and a massive fact: the experience, the fact, of wondering. By wondering about the real, I intend it. I establish and enter into an immediate relation to the real. Moreover, the reach of this wonder cannot be restricted. Try to restrict it, and there will always be someone to wonder whether the restriction holds, and by that very wondering to show that it does not. Further, it is simply futile to suppose that one may wonder about the real without ever attaining it, for if the case for that proposal were made, the real would have been attained at least by that proposal. Fear that the real might be unattainable is, then, self-reversing and groundless. Questions intend not nothing, but everything; not nothing, but being; not some modes and spheres of being, but all its modes and spheres. Questions intend the real, and true answers attain it.

If this summary, spare as it doubtless is, hits off significant moments in common human experience, it follows that we are in possession of resources having far-reaching significance. There are not only two stages in our grasp of the real – that of childhood's grasp of the world through sense perception and that of the age of reason's grasp of the world through evidence, or sufficient reason; there are two options that we confront as theorizing adults. If knowing is sensing, the real is the world that we sense; and if, having thus regressed in theory to the world of childhood, we decide to compensate by becoming 'rigorous', we may conclude that there is no world but the world that we sense.

If, however, knowing is more than sensing, if it comprises wondering, and questioning, and question-answering, and answer-checking, the real is what emerges from those answers that check out. It is the intelligently grasped and reasonably affirmed (where the meaning of 'intelligently' and 'reasonably' includes: relevantly to the data about which we wondered). This account of knowing is called 'critical realism'. It is realism, but not the realism of the infant child. Its critical component derives from its focus on acts of understanding and judgment.

Now, there is a point to be made about understanding (and it impinges on our understanding of judgment). The point is that understanding is intrinsically hypothetical. It is a matter of interesting answers or bright ideas, but not yet a matter of knowledge. If these answers or ideas are to attain the status of knowledge, they call for a complementary step. That is, they must be reflected upon and, if possible, verified. The 'reflection' in question is the quest of sufficient evidence, and 'verification' is the grasp of evidence as sufficient. Judgment, finally, is the act that, by a kind of spontaneous rational necessity, follows on this grasp of evidence.

Positivists, empiricists, naïve realists, if pressed to give an account of what happens in reading, seem to think that reading is a matter of appropriating the meaning contained in the text. But what is the text, over and above ink-spots on a page? One might object that this is not just ink-spots – it is Thucydides! But R. G. Collingwood observes:

> It is only our historical knowledge which tells us that these curious marks on paper are Greek letters; that the words which they form have certain meanings in the Attic dialect . . .[9]

If we manage to construe these 'curious marks', it is in virtue of resources within ourselves that transcend sensing. It is perfectly true that the text exercises a constant guidance to its own proper construal. But the fact remains that, as greeting our senses, the text is nothing other than 'curious marks on paper'. The supposition that we are getting the meaning 'from the page' and the corresponding ideal of doing so with the utmost self-restraint so as to let Thucydides 'speak for himself' are both illusions. The name that Bernard Lonergan proposes for their source is 'naïve intuitionism' or 'the principle of the empty head'. The principle, he says,

> bids the interpreter forget his own views, look at what is out there, let the author interpret himself. In fact, what is out there? There is just a series of signs. Anything over and above a re-issue of the same signs in the same order will be mediated by the experience, intelligence, and judgment of the interpreter.[10]

The root of this intuitionist fallacy is the reduction of the second type of objectivity mentioned above to the first type; that is, it lies in the reduction of the complex objectivity of fully human knowing to the simple objectivity of sense knowing. 'The principle of the empty head' invites us to treat the intelligent and rational act of reading as if it were reducible to 'seeing what is there to be seen'.

It is a fallacy entirely at one with the notion that 'subjectivity' consists in not seeing what is there, or in seeing what is not there. Are not both faults of the *subject*? The *object* is there to be seen; the *subject* fails to see what is there, or sees what is not there. Subjectivity, then, is the opposite and enemy of objectivity. The more subjective the reader, the less objective the reading.

But all this changes, once the appropriate sense of 'object' and appropriate sense of 'objectivity' are brought to bear on the act of reading. If the object is 'meaning', numerous acts of the subject become absolutely indispensable. Among them are: attending to the ink-spots on the page, to recognize them as signs and decode them; then, as a given word-sequence emerges, to construe it to mean such-and-such. Because reading involves a double decoding (of marks to yield word-sequences, and of these sequences to yield their meaning) the word 'text' is ambiguous; it may be used to refer to the marks or to the word-sequences that they yield when decoded. The word-sequences in any case are pressed to provide clues to the understanding of just what those sequences mean.

Like every act of understanding, this one is hypothetical. But the wonder that is the wellspring of all our fully human knowing pushes us beyond hypothesis to knowledge. Hence the effort so to correlate 'hypotheses' with 'givens' as to determine reflectively whether our effort to understand – to grasp the sense of the word-sequence – is correct. In short, the meaning of the text emerges out of the reader's own resources. The reader, however, does not simply leave it at that. Questions for reflection spontaneously occur: Is this, in fact, the meaning that the text is aiming at? What textual warrants make this meaning probable? With what measure of assurance? Judgment, usually no more than a judgment of probability, follows on this kind of reflection.

The reader's fund of experience and resourcefulness of understanding and hard-won equilibrium of judgment do indeed represent habitual subjective acts. But they represent subjectivity at its finest and most authentic. Utterly requisite to successful reading, they dramatize *the dependence of objectivity on authentic subjectivity*. Objectivity (the sort that is relevant not to the restricted sphere of sense perception, but to that of fully human knowing) is precisely *the fruit* or *product* of authentic subjectivity. This, a basic principle of critical realism, is perhaps the most significant single ascertainment in contemporary hermeneutics.[11]

Insights and oversights in reader-response criticism

As reader-response critics began to develop their critical resources in the mid-1970s, two insights (I said above) emerged as pivotal. The first had to do with dispensing with the author; the second, with replacing the centrality of the text by the centrality of the reader. We shall begin by considering the second.

It was clearly grounded in the recognition of how meaning, merely virtual in the signs that constitute the text, becomes actual in and through the activity of the reader. This recognition was laden with consequence. It grounded the repudiation of certain traits of formalist interpretation. So far as this line of thought impinged on specifically biblical scholarship, it signified a clean break with the sketchy theorizing on meaning to be found in average hermeneutics relating to historical-critical procedures.

The idiom of 'replacing the text', however, is misleading. The text remains central to the reader. It is assuredly no longer understood as a container of meaning that the reader passively takes in. It is understood as an index to meaning that must be actively evoked, construed, articulated from within the reader's resources.

What about the author? Whereas reader-response theorists were explicitly intent on doing away with 'the affective fallacy' (the irrelevance of the effects of the text), they remained perfectly at home with 'the intentional fallacy' (the irrelevance of the intentions of the author). Like the inventors of this so-called fallacy, they understood 'intention' not as realized textually, but as entirely extrinsic to the text. They limited it to the psychology at work as the writer attempted to bring the text to birth – a factor of no further interest once the text was born.

Unhappily, this view turned on an oversight; for, the intended sense is intrinsic to the text. It is the formal cause of that singular configuration which constitutes the text; conversely, it is that to which the singular configuration of the text is the index. 'Intention' in this perspective is by no means irrelevant to reading or interpretation. It is precisely the meaning that specifies the text's individuality. The greater the text, the more pronounced its individuality. There is only one Divine Comedy, one Hamlet, one *cimetière marin*. But if we cherish this individuality, distinctiveness, uniqueness, we are obliged to cherish the intended sense, for (whether one knows it or not or likes it or not) uniqueness and intended sense are precisely one and the same.

A mistaken objectification of the intended sense led reader-response criticism to dismiss it as irrelevant. What ought to have become an extremely fruitful dialectic (subjectivity moving toward authenticity through the dynamic tension between a maximally active reader-response and a passionate dedication to the heuristic ideal of the intended sense), instead became an alluring but painfully one-sided exploration of reader-receptivity, response and inventiveness. There followed a festival of insight, as reader-response theory capitalized on precise, if selective, aspects of what readers spontaneously do, and as reader-response practice demonstrated a remarkable *esprit de finesse* on the part of sophisticated, 'competent', and 'at-home' readers.

To say that reader-response theory has had a fruitful impact on practice is not to say much, since that holds in some measure for every theory. Still, reader-response criticism has had a more impressive record than contemporary competing movements. If the accent on the reader legitimated exegetical inventiveness, this only underscored a recurrent feature especially of poetic and dramatic texts: the summons to bring the text to semantic realization and completion. Again, attention precisely to *reading* both in its positive scope and in its limits allowed critics to find fault, persuasively, with excesses in structuralist analysis[12] and illusory theses in deconstructionist criticism.[13] If, on the one hand, historical-critical work often left an impression of banality – monophonic interpretation of polyphonic texts – reader-response criticism often gave the contrary impression of an excess of critical resources (e.g., when the implied reader, the inscribed reader, the fictitious reader, the ideal reader, were all distinguished not only from the real reader but from one another) and of readings that outdid in complexity and creativity the texts being read.

The challenge to and the challenge of reader-response criticism

There is an aspect of reading that reader-response critics celebrate: the bare text is mute, like a musical score. To that extent it is intrinsically unrealized. As an orchestra brings the score to realization in a performance, so a reader brings the text to realization in a reading. Grasp of this state of affairs has clearly been a liberating insight to many reader-response critics.

Furthermore, the actual readings of actual readers determine the fate of the text. They say how the text fares in the world and in history. In this sense, the reader is indeed king.

But there is another side to the matter. Consider the muteness and impotence of the text from the standpoint of the writer. The reader, who is king, may also be a dolt. This is the risk inherent in the act of writing, and it is a risk that often gave the ancients pause. Texts looks ever so intelligent, said Socrates, but if one asks them a question they preserve a solemn silence or else 'always say only one and the same thing' (*Phaedrus*, 275D). Unlike living speech, they are helpless. They question the reader only metaphorically. They cannot in a literal sense 'enter into dialogue', calling attention to the earlier but now forgotten passage, the significant but overlooked detail.

Moreover, great texts generate a tradition of interpretation. The tradition may be authentic, representing accumulated insight, great reach, a steady accumulation of insightful adjustments and reinterpretations. But it may also be inauthentic, representing a falling-off, a watering down, a tailoring of the text to the mediocrity of its readers. 'A book is a mirror', said G. C. Lichtenberg. 'If an ass peers into it, you can't expect an apostle to look out.'

So the challenge to literary criticism today is two-edged. To reader-response theory it is the challenge to acknowledge, without qualification, the need of the reader *to measure up* to the text. Since this is anything but easy, it can never be taken for granted. Before truly measuring up to a given text, a given reader might have to undergo a radical long-term personal development, or even the kind of reversal implied by the word 'conversion'. To grasp – really, not just notionally – that what counts is not subjectivity alone but authentic subjectivity, and to appreciate how utterly this excludes the recoil from self-suspicion that has been the bane of the reader-response movement (as of other contemporary movements in literary theory and practice) is to have an inkling of the cost of conversion.

On the other hand, both reader-response theory and reader-response practice pose a series of challenges to historical-critical method. First, there is the challenge to historical-critical exegetes to cut the last of their underground ties with positivism. Second, there is the challenge to attend intensely and consistently to the implied author or the voice of the text, including the illocutionary and perlocutionary dimensions of that voice. Third, there is the challenge to discover, not a plurality of senses, but the fullness, the multidimensionality, of the sense of the text.

Respecting whether the meaning of the text is one or many, old-timers experienced in dealing with serious forms of 'the one and the many' know that the proper tack is to come down hard on both sides and then try, swiftly and earnestly, to explain oneself.

So long as the defining object of interpretation is the intended sense, the sense of the text, however richly layered, is one. Its oneness derives from an intrinsic (namely, the formal) cause of the text: its unifying form, or intention. But besides interpretation in this (the proper) sense, there is the delicate enterprise of ascription (the ascribing of new, unintended meaning to old, well-known texts) which is an art practised all through the history of literature and indispensable to the richness of that history; and the unending task of analysis (literary, rhetorical, historical, sociological, philosophic, psychological, ideology-critical, and so on). The creativity of ascription, and the many facets brought to light by textually-nurtured analytic reflection are open-ended *ad infinitum*.

Notes

1. In the eighteenth century, however, German pietists such as Johann Albrecht Bengel became leaders in historical-critical scholarship in the cause of subverting Spinozan rationalism.

2. Rudolf Bultmann, 'Is Exegesis Without Presuppositions Possible?' and 'The Problem of Hermeneutics', in *New Testament and Mythology and Other Basic Writings*, ed. S. M. Ogden, Philadelphia and London 1984.

3. William K. Wimsatt, Jr, and Monroe C. Beardsley, 'The Intentional Fallacy', in Wimsatt and Beardsley, *The Verbal Icon*, New York 1958.

4. Wimsatt and Beardsley, 'The Affective Fallacy', in *The Verbal Icon* (n.3).

5. E. D. Hirsch, Jr, *Validity in Interpretation*, New Haven 1967. Hirsch, however, failed to insist on the intended sense as textually objectified.

6. Wayne C. Booth, *The Rhetoric of Fiction*, Chicago 1961, 71.

7. The terms derive from J. L. Austin, *How To Do Things with Words*, ed. J. O. Urmson, Oxford 1962.

8. Bernard Lonergan's adroit, technical formulation of 'sufficient evidence' is 'the virtually unconditioned'. See Lonergan, *Insight*, London 1957, reprinted 1983, 280f.; 343–5; *Method in Theology*, London 1972, 102.

9. R. G. Collingwood, *The Idea of History*, Oxford: 1949, 244.

10. Bernard Lonergan, *Method in Theology* (n.8), 157.

11. The theme is fully spelt out in Bernard Lonergan, 'The Subject', in Lonergan, *A Second Collection*, ed. W. F. J. Ryan and B. J. Tyrrell, London 1974, 69–86: 76–9.

12. See, for example, the criticism, as irrelevant, of structures that the reader cannot be expected to register: Michael Riffaterre, 'Describing Poetic Structures: Two Approaches to Baudelaire's "Les Chats"', in *Reader-Response Criticism*, ed. Jane P. Tompkins, Baltimore and London 1980, 26–40.

13. See, for example, the insistence that 'reference' is in fact indispensable even to texts of that master of intertexuality, James Joyce: Valentine Cunningham, 'Renoving that Bible: The Absolute Text of (Post) Modernism', in *The Theory of Reading*, ed. Frank Gloversmith, Sussex 1984, 1–51.

The Call of Abraham as Read by Jews and Christians

Albert van der Heide

Abraham's call – merit or task?

When in Genesis 12 Abraham is called by God to go out from his land, he is not unknown to the reader of the Bible. In the preceding text there has been mention of his descent and of members of his family. There we also find a brief prelude to Abraham's departure which has always posed problems to exegetes. Already before Abraham's call, his father Terach had journeyed in the direction of Canaan, but had stopped half-way and died in Haran. This fact puts an extra question-mark over the account of the call and stresses the question with which we shall be mainly occupied here. On what basis did Abraham, of all people, get this command and why did he obey it so promptly? What made Abraham, on the basis of a single incident, the model of obedience and trust?

The Bible itself gives a number of motives. The first is the most important and at the same time also stands apart. Directly after the command to leave land and people comes the promise that Abraham himself will become a great people (v.2), a people to whom all other peoples will be directed (v.3). This promise is confirmed for the future with the giving of the land (v.7). It will remain the fixed motif of the stories of Abraham, Isaac and Jacob, and will be supplemented with the making of the covenant and sealed with circumcision. The covenant establishes a mutual relationship between God and Abraham and in so doing lays a great responsibility on Abraham's shoulders.

But the motive of the promise is only an answer to the question of the reason for Abraham's obedience. After all, obedience on the basis of a promise can be motivated by self-interest and longing for glory and greatness. But Abraham put his trust in the one who made him the promise, and when protracted childlessness led him to doubt, he could again manage to believe in God's word and accept the comparison between the starry heaven and his descendants (Gen. 16). So it was not only the promise and the obligations of the covenant which made him obey.

We shall go on to investigate in what ways content is given to the biblical suggestion of Abraham's particular character. First I shall mention some biblical themes and then see how the Christian and Jewish traditions have built on them.

Abraham's belief in the trustworthiness of God's word is soon explicitly mentioned by the biblical narrative itself. His faith is reckoned to him as righteousness (Gen. 15.6; cf. Neh. 9.8). There is also an indication of Abraham's obedience when he is called a servant of the Lord (Gen. 26.24; cf. Ps. 105.6), or when in another connection there is an emphasis on his fear of God (Gen. 22.12). In addition to that we have the striking 'Abraham, my friend' (Isa. 41.8; cf. II Chron. 20.7), where the participle (*ohavi*) in the middle leaves it open whether it is Abraham who loves God or God who loves Abraham – a detail which will concern us later.

Along with the sober narration of the stories about Abraham's life, these detached expressions give us a glimpse of a cautious filling in of his character by the Bible itself, to make it understandable why the command and the promises were given particularly to him. At the same time these sparse facts teach us that the question is not answered by the Bible itself.

Moreover it is not surprising that the traditions which developed on the basis of the biblical facts went further here. They developed the image of Abraham and showed interest in the question why precisely this descendant of Shem and Heber was chosen for this mission. These traditions were selective in their use of the biblical motifs and added their own accents.

I shall next look briefly at the Christian colouring of the picture of Abraham. Then I shall discuss the Jewish picture of Abraham in more detail. I shall leave the image of Abraham in Islam completely out of account.

The Christian Abraham

In the Christian tradition the image of Abraham is primarily determined by two passages from the New Testament: the list of the witnesses of faith in Hebrews 11, and Paul's view of the nature of Abraham's faith in Romans 4.

It is not without significance that Abraham is the Old Testament figure who is mentioned most in the New Testament. The earliest Christian community could see the new beginning represented by Abraham's call as a parallel to its own situation. This precedent in the old covenant lent attraction and legitimacy to the beginning of the Christian community, but at the same time it made Abraham's call seem provisional, pointing forward to its fulfilment in the New Testament. In Acts 7 Stephen puts this emphasis on the history of salvation. He makes it begin with the call of Abraham and stresses the provisional character of the promise of the land: 'Yet he gave him no inheritance in it, not even a foot's length, but promised to give it to him in possession and to his posterity after him, though he had no child. And God spoke to this effect, that his posterity would be aliens in a land belonging to others . . .' (vv.5f.). At the same time we note that Stephen has a solution for the fact that Terach had already gone to Canaan before Abraham received his commission (Gen. 11.31). Against the tendency of the Old Testament text, he attributes both initiatives to Abraham.

Abraham has a comparably important place in Hebrews 11. Throughout this chapter faith is indicated as the power which made him go obediently to the place which he was to receive as an inheritance, so that he went out, not knowing where he was going (v.8). Faith kept him alive in that alien land (v.9), and faith made him obey when he was given the impossible command to sacrifice his only child, who had been given him as the fulfilment of the divine promise (vv.17–18). As an indication of the significance which the author of Hebrews attached to the term faith, we may content ourselves here with his own definition. Faith is 'the assurance of things hoped for, the conviction of things not seen' (v.1). In this connection it is also clear that the power of this inner certainty cannot exclusively be attributed to Abraham. It is the driving force behind all the heroes of the Old Testament.

However, Romans 4 is specifically about Abraham, and there it is also said that Abraham's faith was his most distinctive characteristic. 'Abraham believed God', and even before he had received the sign of circumcision, 'it was reckoned to him as righteousness' (v.3, following Gen. 15.6). Consequently Abraham has become the father of all believers and not just the father of the circumcised (vv. 11–12). Two biblical themes are produced here, covenant and faith. For Paul, faith is clearly the more important, whereas the theme of the covenant takes on a universalistic dimension. Paul is not concerned with Abraham as the first in the specific covenant of circumcision. Abraham, who is also called the father of a multitude of peoples (Gen. 17.4,5), is the father of *all* believers. Here, too, I shall not go into the question of precisely what Paul understood by this faith. But it is clear that it contrasts with obedience to the law and that the essence of it lies in the inner disposition. Paul saw the decisive motive for Abraham's call in this disposition.

This emphasis also remained in later Christian tradition. Abraham is the father of all believers, whose faith is the key for acceptance into the covenant with the God of Israel. In addition there are a number of allegorical and typological motives which stress the spiritual dimension of Abraham's journey. The Septuagint had already sharpened the neutral 'Go from your land' by translating it 'Go out (*exelthe*) from your land', and the Jewish philosopher Philo had already read into this the duty of all believers to leave the old behind them, to be converted and follow the will of God. The church fathers made it an image of following Jesus. The land of the Chaldaeans symbolized pagan astrology, from which Abraham distanced himself.

This short survey may be enough to indicate that Christian readers above all recognized Abraham's disposition as the most important motive for his calling. This disposition is the disposition of a faith which is not dependent on actions and claims, but accepts the invisible as true. In connection with the universalistic character of Christianity, Christians stressed Abraham's significance for all peoples.

The Jewish Abraham

In the Jewish views of Abraham the accents unmistakably lie elsewhere. Because the Jewish tradition tends to be very creative with the open spaces in the Bible, it is impossible to attach the Jewish image of Abraham to a single motif. But there are certainly clear contours. The main motif is not Abraham's faith as an inner certainty of the trustworthiness of God's promises, but an obedience which is evident from his actions. Abraham's significance as the father of all believers certainly plays a part here, but it is less prominent. Abraham's disposition is certainly taken into account, but it is a disposition which is acquired through knowledge and experience.

The most authoritative collection of midrash on the book of Genesis therefore does not disappoint us when we open it at Gen. 12.1 to see the motives that the rabbis conjectured behind the call of Abraham:

Rabbi Yitzhak said: 'Hear, O daughter, consider and incline your ear, forget your people and your father's house' (Ps. 45.11).

Rabbi Yitzhak said: After he [Abraham] had gone from place to place, he saw a castle brightly lit. He said [to himself]: Would you say that a castle [like this] had no lord? The lord of the castle looked out and said to him: I am the lord of the castle. So too it was when our father Abraham said: Would you say that the world had no governor? Then the Holy One looked down and said to him: I am the governor, the Lord of the whole world, 'Let the king delight in your beauty', to make you beautiful in the eyes of all the world, 'for he is your Lord, bow before him' (Ps. 45.12). 'And God said to Abraham: go out of your land . . .' (Bereshit Rabba 39.1, translation p.313. For the references see the bibliography).

This simple similitude speaks of an intuitive knowledge of God on the part of Abraham, which led God to reveal himself to him. This two-sidedness, with a stress on Abraham's role, forms the nucleus of all the Jewish explanations of Abraham's approachability. Here it was a common move to contrast him with his contemporaries and his closest family, who were all stubborn idolaters, and his insight takes on miraculous features.

How old was Abraham when he came to know his creator? Rabbi Hananiah said: He was one year old when he came to know his creator. Rabbi Levi said in the name of Rabbi Simeon ben Lakish: He was three years old, for it says: 'Because (*ekev*) Abraham hearkened to my voice and observed my ordinances: my commandments, my instructions and my laws' (Gen. 26.5). Why *ekev*? The numerical value of that word is 70 + 100 + 2 (*ayin, goph, bet*). Abraham lived for 175 years (Gen. 25.7), and so we learn that he was only three years old when he came to know his creator and that he even observed the details of the Torah (Bereshit Rabbah 95.2, translation pp.882f.; cf. 30.8, translation p.236, where a period of 48 years is mentioned).

Such details are characteristic of the Jewish stories about Abraham. One well-known legend is that of Nimrod, which tells us of the other side of Abraham's lonely spiritual adventure in a world which had been cut off from the true knowledge of God. Here we see the consequences of Abraham's active appearance as the opponent of idolatry.

Rabbi Hiyya said: Terach was a servant [and seller] of idols. Once he went elsewhere and put Abraham as seller in his place. A buyer came who said to him [Abraham]: How old are you? He replied: Fifty. He said: How tragic it is that a fifty-year old should worship a thing of one day! Then he was ashamed of himself and went his way. Once a woman came to him carrying a measure of fine flour. She said to him: Offer this to them as a sacrifice. He stood up and took a stick, smashed the idols to pieces and put the stick in the hands of the biggest of them. When his father came home, he said to him. Who has done that? He said: Why should I deny it? A woman came with a measure of fine flour and said to me: Sacrifice this to them. One said: I shall eat it first, and the other said: No, I shall eat it first. Then this big one stood up, took the stick and smashed them to pieces. He said to him: Don't try to fool me. These idols can't do that sort of thing. He said to him: Can you hear what you are saying? He seized him and took him to Nimrod. Nimrod said to him: Let us worship fire. But he [Abraham] replied: No, let us worship water which can quench fire. Then he said: So let us worship water. But he said: Let us worship the clouds which bear water. He said: Let us worship the clouds. But he said: Let us worship the wind that drives the clouds. He said: Then let us worship the wind. But he said: Let us worship the people who endure the wind. He said: You talk a great deal. We shall worship only fire and I shall have you thrown into it. Then may the God whom you worship come and save you from it (Bereshit Rabba 38.13 in a somewhat free translation, translation pp.31f.).

We find a necessary addition in the Talmud, where the fact of Abraham's unique presence in the world from that moment is used to good purpose:

When the evil Nimrod cast our father Abraham into the fiery oven, Gabriel said to the Holy One: Lord of the world, let me descend and cool the [fire], so that I can rescue this righteous man from the fiery oven. But the Holy One said to him: Just as I am the only one in my world, so he is the only one in his world. It is better for the Only One to save the one. But because the Holy One does not will to fail any single creature, he said: It shall be your part to rescue the children of his children (Hananiah, Mishael and Azariah) (Pesachim 118a, bottom. Cf. Pirqe de Rabbi Eliezer, par. 26 beginning; translation p. 188).

Another haggadic motif that determined the Jewish image of Abraham is of a universalistic kind. Abraham was in no way inclined to keep his knowledge of God to himself. The rather remarkable expression in Gen. 12.5, 'The souls that he had made in Haran', which probably refers to the getting of slaves or another increase in the members of his household, was interpreted by the rabbis as an expression of his first attempts to make proselytes. Even after he had been given the promise that he himself would become a great people, Abraham's zeal for conversion was exemplary. The means he used was hospitality.

'You shall love the Lord your God . . .' (Deut. 6.5). Make him beloved among your fellow men, as your father Abraham did, for it is said: 'And the souls that he had made in Haran' (Gen. 12.5). Is it not the case that if all the inhabitants of the world could come together to create a flea and give it a soul, they could not do it? But this verse teaches that our father Abraham converted them and brought them under the wings of the divine presence (Sifre 32, p.54; translation p.81. Cf. Bereshith Rabba 39.14; translation p.324).

'And Abraham planted an *eshel* in Beer Sheba [and called there on the name of the Lord, the God of the world]' (Gen. 21.33) . . . Rabbi Judah and Rabbi Nehemiah, one said; [*Eshel* is] a garden; the other said, an inn. Resh Lakish said: That teaches us that our father Abraham made anyone who came by call on the name of the Holy One. How did he do that? After they had eaten and drunk, they rose up to thank him. Then he said: Do any of you think that you have eaten at my expense? You have eaten at the expense of the Lord of the world. Praise him and give him thanks, he who spoke and brought the world into being (Sota 10a/b. Cf. Bereshit Rabba 49.4; translation pp.423–4).

These passages from rabbinic literature show us the way in which the special nature of Abraham is brought out. This phenomenon is not limited to the illustrations that I have cited. The classical rabbinic sources contain more, but there are also earlier and very much later texts on the subject. The book of Jubilees, an early Jewish retelling of part of the biblical history from the second century BCE, stresses Abraham's wisdom and virtue and already makes use of the narrative motives which I have cited here in rabbinic-haggadic garb. The *Book of Biblical Antiquities* which was once attributed to the philosopher Philo (first century BCE), which narrates and interprets part of the biblical history, pays a good deal of attention to Abraham. There he is thrown into the oven because he did not want to have any part in the godless plan to build the tower of Babel. It is important to see that both these early Jewish sources attach great importance to Abraham's actions and to the effective expression of his disposition.

The narrative manner of expressing Abraham's attitude has had a long life. In the early mediaeval so-called Lesser Midrashim there is a loving elaboration above all of the Nimrod affair and Abraham's martyrdom, when he flees, is put in prison and finally thrown into the oven. Still later these stories form part of a vast repertory of narratives, plays and even children's books. In addition to Abraham's martyrdom, considerable attention was also paid to the miracle of his intuitive knowledge of God and the stories of how he acquired this at a very early age.

But the Jewish tradition was not just concerned with Abraham in a narrative way. Abraham was also a great model for philosophers and theologians, and at the level of theological reflection, too, his way to the true knowledge of God was a source of inspiration. I can only give a glimpse of this.

The tone is set by Moses Maimonides (1138–1204), when in his great legal codex he describes the origin and background of idolatry:

2. . . . In the course of time the venerable and terrible Name was forgotten by all the living beings and no one still knew him, so that ordinary men, women and children knew nothing but the forms of wood and stone and the stone temples in which they had grown up from

childhood, to which they bowed down, which they worshipped, and by which they swore. And the wise men among them, like the priests and suchlike, imagined that there was no other divinity than the stars and the heavenly spheres and that the images were made to depict these. But no one knew the Rock of Eternity and only a few in the world knew of him, like Enoch, Methuselah, Noah, Shem and Heber. And in this way the world went on, until the pillar of the world was born, that is, our father Abraham.

3. When this eternal citizen of the world had outgrown his mother's womb, he began to search restlessly in his spirit. Little as he was, he began to reflect day and night, and he was bewildered that it was possible for our heaven continually to rotate when there was no one to propel it and make it go round, and it was impossible for it to propel itself. Without a teacher or anyone to explain he was buried in Ur of the Chaldaeans among the foolish star-worshippers, where his father and mother and everyone else worshipped the stars and he joined in with them. But his heart was restless and sought understanding, until he attained the way of truth and came to understand the fact of righteousness from his own true capacity for understanding. He knew that there is one Godhead which moves the heavenly sphere and who created all things, and that there is no other Godhead than he in all the being that is. He knew that the whole world was steeped in folly and that what led people to this folly was that they worshipped the stars and the images, so that their sense of the truth had been lost. In the fortieth year of his life Abraham came to know his creator. When he had arrived at this insight, he began to argue with the inhabitants of Ur and to challenge them by saying: The way that you are taking is not that of the truth. He broke the idols in pieces and he began to proclaim to the people that only the God of the world is deserving of worship and that one may bow down to him, offer him sacrifices and libations, so that all creatures to come shall know him, and that it is appropriate to destroy and to break all idols, so that not all the people should end up in folly, as those who imagine that there are no other gods than these. When his arguments convinced them, the king tried to kill him, but a miracle happened to him and he went to Haran. There he began to proclaim with great insistence to everyone that in all the world there is only one God and that men may worship him. So he went around and summoned the people from city to city and from kingdom to kingdom, till he came to the land of Canaan, and there too cried out, as it is written: 'And there he called on the name of the Lord, the God of the world' (Gen. 21.33). And when the people gathered around him and asked about his words, he proclaimed to each one of them in accord with his understanding,

until he had brought them back to the way of truth and had gathered thousands and ten thousands around him, the men of Abraham's house. He planted this great truth in their heart, and in addition he wrote books about it and handed them on through his son Isaac . . . (Maimonides, *Mishneh Torah*. Hilchot Avodat Kochavim I.2–3, pp.72–3. Here Abraham's age is perhaps deliberately put at the significant figure of forty).

In addition to the fact that here Maimonides gives a summary of the most important themes of the classical rabbinic sources about the significance of Abraham, one element is stressed: Abraham had sought and found, he acquired understanding of the fact of righteousness by virtue of his own capacity for understanding, *mitevunato na-nekhona*, so that he knew that there was one God to whom alone worship is due. Elsewhere Maimonides puts it like this:

When the pillar of the world grew up and it became clear to him that there is a God existing by himself who is not a body nor an embodied force, and that all the stars and spheres are made by him, and when he began to understand that the things in which he had been brought up were folly, he began to refute their teaching and to show that their views were false. He publicly proclaimed his dissident views and 'called on the name of the Lord, the God of the world' (Gen. 21.33); this implies [faith in] the existence of the deity and of the creation of the world (*Guide to the Perplexed* III.29, translation p.516).

For Maimonides, this fact of accepting the existence and unity of God with understanding is the great truth, *ha-iggar ha-gadol*, and the first command of the Torah (cf. *Mishneh Torah*, Hilchot Jesode ha-Tora I.1, translation p.1). The example of Abraham is so important because it indicates that it is possible for an elect individual to perform this great commandment, even without prior instruction on the basis of tradition or revelation. An innate receptivity to the true knowledge of God that one develops by the means of philosophical contemplation is a human characteristic. And Abraham not only found the beginning of this path, but also followed it to the end. Abraham's piety was the true piety that is based on love, which does not need God for hope of reward or fear of punishment, but solely on the basis of innate need and burning love (cf. *Mishneh Torah*, Hilchot Teshuva X.2, translation p.134).

Maimonides' positive look at the possibility of intuitive knowledge of God is a self-conscious expression of the most important motive in the parable of the illuminated castle which we found in Bereshit Rabba. However, other Jewish theologians too do not neglect to stress the opposite motif. Jehuda ha-Levi (1075–c.1141) is a well-known representative of a trend which saw philosophical contemplation as being at best half the story. For him, too, Abraham had certainly got a long way in his own power, but the crown of his search had to be given to him. The true knowledge of God is indeed based on love of God; it is the stage at which the human spirit is overwhelmed by the superior power of divine love, and in which it leaves behind its own efforts as futile and inadequate (for this see Kuzari I V.27, translation p.240; I V16–17, translation p.223).

Here we perceive a question which will certainly seem familiar to us. For Maimonides, the way to God is a way of ascent, which can only be travelled by an individual to the end but which nevertheless lies before us as a challenge. In Jehuda ha-Levi, Abraham can achieve the true knowledge of God only on God's own initiative. What is still held together in the simple rabbinic parable has diverged in these later thinkers into two different answers to the question of the presence of God and the possibility of knowing him in a world which has forgotten him.

Finally I want to stress another element from the Abraham tradition which in my view gives an extra dimension to Abraham's call. It is that of the Ten Trials of Abraham.

The idea that in his life Abraham had to undergo a number of trials and that he withstood them all is a very old one. We already find it clearly mentioned in the book of Jubilees, which I mentioned earlier (17.17; 19.8). The number of these trials has been schematically set at ten. In rabbinic literature there is no complete agreement on the question as to which events in Abraham's life can be reckoned in this series of trials. In its most elementary form, the tradition is placed among another series of tens from salvation history:

> With ten trials was our father Abraham tested and he withstood them all, to show us how great was the love of our father Abraham (Aboth V.3).

Here we note that from the context it is no longer clear that Abraham's love of God is meant; some prefer the view that this passage is about God's love for Abraham.

What trials are these? In the book of Jubilees, the call of Abraham is mentioned as the first trial; the sacrifice of Isaac is the ninth and the death and burial of Sarah the tenth. By contrast, the rabbinic traditions all agree that the sacrifice of Isaac was the conclusion of the series. Episodes from Abraham's youth are put at the beginning, but Maimonides says very firmly:

> The ten trials by which Abraham was proved are all in scripture. The first was his becoming an alien on the command of God: 'Go from your

land . . .' [there follows a complete summary]. The tenth was the binding of Isaac (*Commentary on the Mishnah*, Aboth V.3; text in the current editions of the Talmud. For a completely worked-out series see Pirqe de-Rabbi Eliezer, paras. 26–31; translation pp.187–230; there is a shorter and different series in Avot de Rabbi Nathan, A 33.2, p.94, translation p.132).

So Maimonides suggests a parallel between Gen. 12 and Gen. 22, the call and the sacrifice. It is certainly no coincidence that Maimonides has chosen this way out of the dilemma of competing rabbinic traditions. There is more that points in this direction. The striking similarity in the wording of the command offers a first point of contact. The Midrash takes it up like this:

> Rabbi Levi said: Twice there is written 'Go' (*Lech lecha*), but we do not know which of the two is the more precious, the first or the second. Rabbi Johanan said: 'Go out of your land', that is your province, 'and from the place of your birth', that is your district, 'and from your fathers' house', that is just the parental house, 'to the land that I shall show you.' Why did he not reveal that straightaway? To make it more precious in his eyes and to give him a reward for each step. That is the view of Rabbi Johanan, for Rabbi Johanan also said: 'Take your son.' Which son? 'Your only son.' Both are the only sons of their mother. 'Whom you love.' I love both of them. He said to him, 'Isaac.' And why did he not reveal it to him straightaway? To make him precious in his eyes and to give him the reward for each command separately. For Rabbi Huna says in the name of Rabbi Eliezer: Just as the Holy One holds the righteous in tension and only later reveals to them the reasons for a matter, so we also find, 'To the land that I shall show you' (Gen. 12.1), 'On one of the mountains that I shall show you' (Gen. 22.2) (Bereshit Rabba 39.9, translation p.318).

This fragment indicates the most important agreements between the two commands and gives them meaning. But there are more parallels between the narratives of the first and last direct encounters between God and Abraham. In both there is a very incisive command to set out on a journey the destination of which is not given.

Just as in Gen. 12 Abraham has to part from the family which was before him, so in Gen. 22 he must part, as it were, from the family which is to come after him. In both stories the conclusion is the offering of a sacrifice on an altar which he himself has built (12.8; 22.9, 13), and which in both cases is linked with a repetition of the promise of the land and the blessing of a great people (12.7, which takes up vv.2–3; 22.17–18). This modest parallel between the two stories is support for the notion that Abraham's life was surrounded by a series of trials. Abraham's call was the beginning of a long road. To the triumphalistic conceptions of the successful hero of faith who knows God is now added the theme of the one who is subjected to trial, who withstands the test, but is immediately tested again in a series which will end up in the severest trial conceivable in the life of Abraham: the confrontation with a God who denies his own promise and trust. The glorious victory of Nimrod and his foolish idolaters is forgotten. Abraham is no longer the protagonist. 'With ten trials was our father Abraham tested, to show us how great was the love of God had for Abraham' (Aboth V.3). God stands centre stage. And because God loved Abraham, he tested him time and again, for 'the reward accords with the difficulty' (Aboth V.23). God himself chooses whom he will put to the test.

> 'The Lord tests the righteous' (Ps. 11.5). Rabbi Jonathan said: A potter does not test the pots which do not look so good, since you need only to give a tap to break them. But how does he test them? With the good, stout pots, which you can strike a number of times without their breaking. So too the Holy One does not test the godless, but the righteous, as it is written, 'The Lord tries the righteous' (Bereshit Rabba 55.2, translation p.482).

Two different views of Abraham's call are kept in equilibrium. The strong, successful hero who does not fail in anything points forward to the weary old warrior, who must desperately gird himself in armour for the umpteenth time and go out to fight for his king.

> Rabbi Simeon bar Abba said: 'Will you take your son . . .' (Gen. 22.2); this is formulated as a request. It can be compared with a king who had had to wage many wars and who had a heroic warrior who had won them all. Finally he confronted the decisive battle and said to him: Please also stand fast in this battle, so that my enemies may not be able to say that the first victories did not mean anything. So too God spoke to Abraham: I have tried you many times and you have always stood the test. Stand fast now, so that people shall not be able to say, The first trials did not mean anything (Sanhedrin 89b).

This last passage reflects the dialectic of Abraham's merit. In the last resort the initiative in what takes place between human beings and heaven cannot come from one side. The Caller needs someone to call and the Tester needs someone to test. Certainly everything is in the hands of heaven, but the fear of heaven is not (cf. Berachot 33b).

The open character of many of the biblical narratives compels the readers to fill them in. If the Bible leaves the occasion for the call of Abraham uncertain, the rabbinic tradition at first sight fills in the image of Abraham in quite a robust way. It is characteristic of the Jewish tradition that this picture acquires additions and nuances which give it a depth comparable to the depth of rabbinic thought itself.

Translated by John Bowden

Bibliographical postscript

General
One gets a good idea of the variety of the legends about Abraham from L. Ginzberg, *The Legends of the Jews*, Philadelphia 1909–38, reprinted New York 1970, Vol. 1. pp. 271–86, and the relevant notes in Vol. 5.

Other texts mentioned
Jubilees: O. S. Wintermute, 'Jubilees. A new translation and introduction', in J. H. Charlesworth (ed.), *The Old Testament Pseudepigrapha* II, New York and London 1985, 35–142.

Book of Biblical Antiquities: D. J. Harrington and J. Cazeaux, *Pseudo–Philon: Les Antiquités Bibliques* I, Introduction et texte critique, traduction, Paris 1976; M. R. James, *The Biblical Antiquities of Philo*, London 1917, reprinted with an extended preface by L. H. Feldman, New York 1971.

Lesser Midrashim: A. Jellinek, *Bet ha-Midrasch*, Jerusalem 1967 (on Abraham, Vol. I, pp.25–34, 43–46; Vol. II, pp.118–19; Vol. V, pp.40–41); A. Wünsche, *Aus Israels Lehrhallen. Kleine Midrashim und spätere legendarische Literatur des Alten Testaments*, Leipzig 1907–10 (I, p.14–18: German translation of the Abraham stories).

Rabbinic texts quoted (the renderings are all my own). Passages from the Mishna and Talmud can be found in I. Epstein (ed.), *The Babylonian Talmud*, London 1948–52 (text and English translation).

Aboth de Rabbi Nathan: S. Schechter (ed.), *Aboth de Rabbi Nathan*, Vienna 1887, reprinted Hildesheim 1979; J. Goldin, *The Fathers according to Rabbi Nathan*, New Haven 1955 (English translation of version A).

Bereshith Rabba: J. Theodor and C. Albeck, *Bereschit Rabba*, Jerusalem 1965; H. Freedman and M. Simon, *Midrash Rabbah* I–II: *Genesis*, London and Bournemouth 1951 (English translation).

Pirqe de Rabbi Eliezer: G. Friedlander, *Pirke de Rabbi Eliezer. The Chapters of Rabbi Eliezer the Great*, translated and annotated, London 1916, reprinted New York, etc. 1965. *Sifre*: L. Finkelstein (ed.), *Sifre on Deuteronomy*, New York 1969; H. Bietenhard, *Der tannaitische Midrasch Sifre Deuteronomium*, translated with commentary, Bern, etc. 1984.

Mediaeval

Judah Halevi, *An Argument for the Faith of Israel. The Kuzari*. Translated from the Arabic by H. Hirschfeld, London 1905, reprinted New York 1964.

Moses Maimonides: H. M. Russell and J. Weinberg, *The Book of Knowledge from the Mishnah [!] Torah of Maimonides*, translated from the Hebrew, Edinburgh 1981 and New York 1983; S. Pines, *The Guide of the Perplexed*, Chicago 1963, reprinted 1974.

II · Historical Perspectives

The Bible as Read in the Early Church: Patristic Exegesis and its Presuppositions

Charles Kannengiesser

1. Scripture divine

The first and most fundamental of all presuppositions regulating patristic exegesis was to consider Scripture as *divine*. Holy Writ provided an access to God, a way of communicating with God, which was in itself a divine disposition. There was no question that God ultimately was the source of the Book, deciding about its content and authorizing its relevance. Between the rabbi Trypho and the Christian philosopher Justin, in the middle of the second century, a common ground for discussion was provided by their shared admission of the scripture's *divine* nature. The church had introduced no innovation in regard to such an assumption when identifying herself as an autonomous body of believers separated from the synagogue. The radical shift in hermeneutics inaugurated by Paul the apostle created the novelty of a christological focus in a pre-established recognition of *divine* scripture. The same sacred character of scripture was still presupposed, over half a millenium later, in the more narrative and popular use of it by Gregory the Great.

As a privileged access to God, itself managed by divine means such as direct inspiration, supernatural dictation, vision, or prophecy, Holy Writ allowed a unique symbiosis between its transcendent locutor and addresses. The message was the living word of God in a written form; it changed the lives of its receivers. It was not only a canonized relic from older times, it was a powerful presence of the inspiring Spirit, ready to operate in the midst of the faithful community. Therefore the relevance of scripture was not perceived as a theoretical norm, as a matter of principle;

it was experienced immediately in liturgical action and private prayer. In any case, exegesis presupposed the ordinary Christian's existential familiarity with scripture from the earliest stage of the preparation to baptism on. Being seen as of a divine authorship and received as a life-saving instruction, Holy Writ overpowered any human authority in the church. In order to build up the latter, to let an ecclesiastical self-definition grow out of the disputes and the confusions inevitable in the first days of what became the Christian movement, divine scripture served as the sole warrant of an authentic faith in Christ. The new hermeneutics, proper to the nascent church, interpreted scripture's divine truth in letting Christ's voice announce in it, or proclaim and statute, all that was vital for Christians in their present experience of the world. God was identified, outside any metaphysics, in the terms of scripture, and the same God was in the present introducing chosen believers into the salvific disposal secured by Holy Writ.

One could add endless remarks of that sort that would serve to underline the basic patristic presupposition on which Christian exegesis rested from its very birth on: scripture is *divine*.

2. Scripture ecclesiastical

Another basic category determined the birth and all the subsequent developments of patristic exegesis: scripture makes sense only when interpreted *in* and *for* the church. In short, scripture is *ecclesiastical*.

In the light of the gospel's original conviction, Holy Writ as a whole carried on a highly needed understanding about Christ. Christological data, discovered by the earliest interpreters of scripture in the church of the New Testament, validated a *Christian* appropriation of the Hebrew Bible. The latter's *divine* nature was thoroughly understood as *Christian*. History and culture, independently from the emergence of the Christian movement during the first century CE, imposed also that scripture was to be received by the first Christians in its Greek edition. The *hebraica veritas* of scripture would become a critical norm much later, first for the great Origen in third-century Alexandria, and, in the late fourth century, for his ungrateful disciple, the Latin intellectual Jerome. In the spontaneous reception of Holy Writ by the earliest Christian generations, it made no difference to read the Greek Septuagint rather than the Torah written in Hebrew, at least in so far as the *divine* nature of scripture was concerned. The collection of sacred books differed, not their supernatural relevance.

The full set of Old and New Testament writings was received by the many Christian groups, spread over vast regions of the Roman Empire. It constituted, near the end of the second century, the innermost treasure of the church, her heart and soul. The canonical definition and counting of those writings was the result of a long and complex process, called the 'formation of the canon'. As a result of that process there are gospels, and epistles, or apocalypses categorized as canonical or non-canonical. The criterion of orthodoxy was added to the distinction thus made.

It was quite clear in the view of Irenaeus, in the late second century, or of the African Tertullian one generation later, that the dramatic struggle for establishing a correct set of canonical books made sense only if those books were already the property of the church. Belonging to a group which claimed to be the church entailed the responsibility for the preservation and safe transmission of Holy Writ, at the core of the community's daily life. In periods of persecution, one of the worst cases of betrayal was to hand the sacred books over to civil authorities.

Not only was Holy Writ as such considered to be entrusted by God to the church, it was also declared to be the church's primary message. In fact, what the church had to announce was scripture; and what the whole of scripture articulated in a divine way was the church. Patristic exegesis would play from century to century with the interferences of those two hermeneutical levels of Christian identification. The basic principle of the initial reception and of later interpretations of Holy Writ in the church was always the same: Holy Writ is *ecclesiastical* by its very nature. Scripture made sense in Christian terms, *because* it was proper to nascent Christianity, not *in order to* contribute to it. Holy Writ, as bestowed on the church, deserved to be given entirely to each church member. There was never an inner circle in Christian communities, with an esoteric use of the Bible, at least not during the patristic era. Inner circles of interpreters flourished here and there, but no Christian was ever deprived of the symbolic possession and personal appropriation of Holy Writ as such. Therefore, patristic exegesis resulted in a staggering amount of sermons and other essays, distributed to church people.

It is worth exploring a little more some implications of the basically *ecclesiastical* orientation of patristic exegesis.

In negative terms, the exegesis of scripture in the early church never meant a scientific study limited to a circle of experts. It was not considered a scholastic task, or a learned discipline separated from others in the fixed curriculum of an academic institution. It was not a secular enterprise which regarded biblical writings as any other literary legacy. Even when using methods and criteria applied by contemporary non-Christian interpreters to classical sources of Hellenic traditions, patristic exegetes never intended to assimilate the Bible to their classical heritage. They did not allegorize *Kings* or *Chronicles* as another *Iliad* nor did they identify

Abraham's journey and Moses' long-lasting exodus as a variant of the *Odyssey*. Even in the framework of the Judaeo-Christian tradition, patristic exegesis never admitted a neutral form of collaboration between scholars of dissenting communities, much less between rabbis and Christian experts. No interest was developed in Hebrew scripture as proper to Judaism, nor was the Old Testament scrutinized independently from the New.

In positive terms, the ecclesiastical nature of patristic exegesis called for intellectual leaders who served exclusively their church communities. With their fellow Christians, such leaders shared a firmly regulated group experience. The Bible circulated in all circumstances of community life. The Bible was the very matrix out of which the group generated its own idiom, as one may still observe today in the Southern 'Bible Belt' of the United States. Nothing illustrated more the interaction between scripture and indigenous language, during the first centuries, than the constant interpolation of biblical phrases into the parlance of the day. A Christian Latin emerged out of Tertullian's apologies and of Cyprian's letters, which marked Augustine's style to the point of letting him favour a colloquial paraphrase of scripture in his sermons.

Liturgical gatherings, collective or individual prayer, catechetical procedures, festivals, visits and communications from one group to another, marked the Christian movement in its earliest stages, during the first and the second century CE. As the unique source of divine revelation, the Bible secured the core-regulation of the whole intellectual and institutional structuring of Christian lifestyles.

3. Scripture interpreted

It is time to consider more specifically patristic exegesis in its full historical dimensions. My purpose is not just to describe strictly technical questions. For instance, there has been much discussion in recent decades about allegorism and the so-called 'senses' of scripture proper to biblical exegesis in the early church. I shall not repeat what has become common knowledge, but I will try, rather, to approach the global phenomenon of patristic exegesis in the light of our current attempt to retrieve critically the foundations of Christianity.

In a reflection of these foundations, the very notion of a Christian Bible needs some additional comments. As venerated by later generations of Christians, the Bible did not circulate in the early church for two or three centuries. One must count two centuries if the time needed for the formation of a scriptural canon is considered, or three after several generations of churchmen had struggled with Marcionite reductions of the biblical canon and opposed Gnostic trends hostile to the Old Testament. In other words, the Christian Bible in its making was of top priority in the long drawn-out process of the original identity-quest of the church. Therefore, the Bible was not so much *in* the earliest church as it was allowing the church to *exist*, and to become aware of its proper nature. Hebrew scripture was Christianized through its canonical reception in the version of the Septuagint, which means that the church identified herself as a body of received beliefs and religious practices in line with the ordinances of the Bible. It would be a fatal flaw for today's critics to perceive Bible and early church as two extrapositioned realities. They have never existed independently from each other. There never was a Bible, as known by later generations, outside the church, and there never was a church of any properly Christian foundation without the Bible. A striking illustration of this interaction is to observe how the Christianizing of *Genesis*, from Paul's letters to the *Galatians* and to the *Romans* on, entailed the very genesis of the Christian movement.

The vital link between scripture and early church, thus evidenced, gives enough reason, it seems to me, for introducing patristic exegesis as thoroughly ecclesiastical in its whole *raison d'être*. The church itself, in which patristic exegesis played such a decisive role, needs now to be set in focus. For it is important to keep in view the patristic period as a whole when evaluating patristic exegesis.

A Christian self-understanding, born out of the hermeneutical conversion which had given way to the New Testament, resulted in a reading of scripture as the *Christian* Bible. It is foremost and precisely that reading which gave a proper unity and consistency to the church at large. The scale on which patristic exegesis exercised its integrating power is remarkable. I would dare to claim that it is the dynamic of that exegesis, more than anything else, which made it possible to have the patristic period covering half a millenium of Mediterranean cultures in East and West. More than through political alliances, or thanks to the type of administration inherited from the late Roman empire, a formal unity was warranted between the Christian patriarchates by their common submission to the same divine revelation learned from scripture. In a period running from the second to the seventh century CE, the creative radiance of scripture permeated all traditional values of late antiquity. Maximus Confessor, who died in 662, is witness to a theological synthesis essentially based on scripture. As long as a cultural development was possible in Roman antiquity, the so-called Fathers addressed the *universal* unity of the church as they saw it. From Isidore of Seville (d.636) and John of Damascus (d.749) on, people used to collect testimonies from all past

Christian centuries as from one specific era, until the time when Peter Lombard, in the midst of the twelve century, gave such *Libri Sententiarum* over to the later Middle Ages. In short, patristic exegesis refers to a very complex and long-lasting period of civilization, but which must be considered as foundational for Christian traditions as a whole.

Mistaken as it would be to categorize patristic exegesis in terms of a scholastic discipline, comparable with academic exegesis of today, it would be short-sighted to regard that era of patristic exegesis as a shrunken appendix of the New Testament age. Current Christian ideologies of very diverse provenance seem to have a hard time when facing the early church in its complete significance and chronological extension. In fact, 'early' means here a powerful cultural process covering several centuries. It means a far-flung chorus of schools of thought, from a complexity of human institutions, and in many distinct languages. Christianity, in its seminal inspirations, eventually pervaded the whole texture of society in the patristic period. The epoch-making embodiment of Christian beliefs during those early centuries allows us to verify the true nature of patristic exegesis. For the only 'nuclear' energy in the early church was the spiritual power of scripture, channelled by authorized interpreters and theologians, and dispersed along the many ascetical trends experienced in Christian groups. To choose another metaphor, patristic exegesis is the spinal column of the body of our most ancient past. It is no surprise, then, if these ancient exegetical traditions continue to haunt the 'musée imaginaire' of Christian traditions even today. Not only christological dogma, but all Christian attitudes toward life and death, the whole spectrum of beliefs about heaven and hell, or about the beginnings and the end of times, were shaped by patristic exegesis. Any sacred authority in the Church, or any sacramental practice, from their first articulation, through their consolidation during many centuries of Christian traditions, rest on the basis of patristic exegesis.

We may well conclude our sketchy survey wondering if it is actually possible to underestimate the obvious and central importance of patristic exegesis for the hermeneutic of Christian foundations so badly needed for the Church today.

4. Exegesis without scripture?

Methodologically, patristic exegesis is a phenomenon of the past. Its symbolic reading of scripture, overladen with antiquated cosmological presuppositions, has become foreign to our culture. Not only was it bound to classical languages now cut off from the mainstream of life, but it functioned in the church on the basis of a cultural consensus which no longer exists. On the other hand, patristic exegesis, which regulated faith and order, as well as sacraments and ethics in the ancient church, must be recognized in its own right as belonging to the foundations of Christian traditions. It represents such an amount of literature in Greek, Latin, Syriac, Armenian, Georgian, Coptic, Ethiopian, Old Slavonic, even Old Irish, and Old Germanic, that many of its riches remain unexplored. More than in today's Pompeii there is still a lot to be dug out in the immense field of a millennium of homilies, commentaries and other essays, directly or indirectly inspired by patristic exegesis until the time of Abelard and Bernard of Clairvaux in the twelfth century.

Now we know that a critical archeology of knowledge does not only explore a dead past. It also treats that past as an *arché*, a source of meaning for people alive today. We no longer speak the Greek of the Fathers, even in Greece itself; but the classical heritage remains operative in the whole Western world, from Leningrad to Santa Barbara in Southern California, and from Norway to New Zealand. It would be a case of complete ideological blindness to dismiss the fact that patristic exegesis yields a similar *arché* to contemporary Christianity. Indeed, it offers criteria and insights which are most helpful for reassessing Christian realities. It opens an access to vital foundations, questioned today in the light of many new historical disciplines. It helps theologians to retrieve the treasures of ancient dogmatics, still relevant for the ongoing talk on God. In short, it secures valid principles to anyone who tries to reach a creative self-understanding as a Christian believer. In the acutely modern crisis of the millennium-old Christian traditions, nothing might be more liberating than to gain new insights about the very foundations of those traditions. Such insights are provided by the study of patristic exegesis.

As a practical conclusion, I should observe that my argument does not lead to recommending a return to the exegetical practice of the Fathers. It makes hardly any sense to compare patristic and contemporary exegesis. The former assumes a faithful dedication to the church. Its motivation is doctrinal and apologetic in shifting focuses between the Ten Commandments and the Creed. Its discussion of biblical texts, while bound to the grammar and rhetoric of late antiquity, always serves the purposes of highly spiritual and religiously-minded interpreters. At its best, patristic exegesis communicates more about the church-experience undergone by the exegetes of the second through the seventh century than about data pertaining directly to the sacred text.

Modern exegesis, as a response to the Enlightenment, focuses exclusively on such data. As a discipline, its motivation is no longer theological, nor is its purpose to encounter in scripture the living God. It is a professional exercise of text-criticism and historical inquiry, which dispenses the interpreters from being Christian believers, and omits to address scripture as holy. In short, it is a form of exegesis without scripture. Much needs to be clarified about the status in the church of contemporary exegesis. Being by definition a scholastic business, it leads contemporary exegetes, happily confined in their professional specialities, to declare that patristic exegesis is non-critical and therefore irrelevant for the modern reader of the Bible. At the same time, one would deplore the powerful upsurge of fundamentalistic attitudes, evidenced throughout the different Christian denominations; a non-critical approach to the scriptures by high-levelled officials as well as by the common people in the churches. But fundamentalism is a negative reaction to the challenge of the Enlightenment and as such is nothing but the dark side of an enlightened exegesis which has overcome the challenges of the Enlightenment only to find itself finally trapped in the latter's problematic. Patristic exegesis offers a powerful paradigm in such a case, not as an exegetical alternative, but as an original perception of what being a Christian means in biblical terms.

The Treatment of the Bible in Judaism

Günter Stemberger

In Judaism, exegesis does not begin with the complete, finished text of the Bible; rather, it is the driving force in the development within the Bible, which has constantly taken up earlier sacred traditions anew, adapted them to new situations in life, and made them more profound.

Jewish writings from the time of the Second Temple like the Book of Jubilees, the Genesis Apocryphon from Qumram or Pseudo-Philo's *Book of Biblical Antiquities* essentially deal with the Bible in just the same way as the books of Chronicles deal with their biblical basis in Genesis to II Kings. This is a narrative, accentuating, 'implicit' exegesis, which also supports newer legal and ethical conceptions, in the form of a re-reading, and in a more restrained form it also influences the Septuagint and large parts of Flavius Josephus's *Jewish Antiquities*. Alongside this, however, at an early stage there were also attempts at 'explicit' exegesis, like the allegorical commentary of Philo of Alexandria and above all the Qumran *pesharim*, which interpret the Bible historically in terms of their own time, which is felt to be the end time (here they are similar to the Gospels). Behind them stands the awareness that the authorized exegate is himself as it were inspired, and experiences strata of the biblical text which remained hidden even from the actual prophet. This is said explicitly in the Habakkuk *pesher*.

1. Targum

We also know from Qumran the first examples of the Targum, Aramaic 'translations' of the Bible (in addition to a small piece of Leviticus, above all a Targum on Job). These texts are still very close to the original Hebrew text (in so far as there already was a fixed type of text at that time), providing exegesis only through slight changes, additions, and a particular choice of vocabulary. All the other Targums have been handed down to us only in a later form with a rabbinic stamp, though in individual cases there is considerable dispute over the datings.

If we leave aside the Qumran texts, the aim of which cannot be determined with any certainty, we find the first evidence of the institution of the Targum in the Mishnah. It is part of the worship of the synagogue, directly connected with the reading of scripture, but carefully separated from this. While the ordinary people needed at least a translation into the Aramaic vernacular, the rabbis were aware that no translation can do justice to the text of the revelation. Later tradition put the dilemma of the translator like this: 'Anyone who translates a verse literally is a forger; anyone who adds anything is a blasphemer' (Kiddushin 49a). Therefore so that the Targum should not be understood as part of the revealed Bible, the Mishnah lays down that the person who presents the Targum may not be the one who reads the text of the Bible; nor may he use any written text, so as to exclude any confusion with the written Torah. However, thus safeguarded, the Targumist is given great freedom. His presentation combines translation with an explanation of the scriptural reading which brings it up to date; so it is often almost impossible to distinguish between a Targum and a biblical sermon.

The association between the Targum and worship meant that at an early stage different kinds of Targums were produced, particularly on the first reading, the Pentateuch, and then on the 'scrolls' of Song of Songs, Lamentations, Esther and Ruth, which were read at certain great festivals. By contrast, the prophetic texts, which are so central for the Christian understanding of the Bible, fall somewhat into the background, since they were the second reading (in the Jewish understanding Joshua to II Kings are also part of the prophetic books, the 'former prophets').

Three complete versions of Targums on the Pentateuch have come down to us: Onqelos, Pseudo-Jonathan and Neofiti; in addition, there are various recensions of the so-called Fragment Targum. One can assume that these texts represent only a cross-section of what was originally a far wider spectrum. Ideally, indeed, each targumist in the synagogue presented his own Targum, adapted to the needs of the community. Written texts were only a help and stimulation towards preparation, but where the targumist had no relevant training, he might simply learn a model text off by heart.

As the main task of the translator of the biblical reading was to bring the text up to date and apply it to the situation in his community, written versions of the Targum also had to be constantly adapted afresh. Not only were the contemporary place names put it, but we can see in the biblical text allusions to political conditions (Edom, for example, becomes a cipher for Rome, Ishmael for Islam); above all, theological accents were added (clearly, for example, in the commentary-translation of Gen. 22, the story of sacrifice of Isaac, which was central to Jewish religious feeling).

As the influence of the rabbinate on the life of the community became increasingly strong, and with it attempts developed to control the Targum theologically, probably many motives from the Midrash were taken into the Targum. We cannot always be certain whether the Midrash has taken something from the Targum tradition or vice versa, but usually we should assume the former possibility.

The constant updating of the Targum, which only ceases in the Middle Ages with the disappearance of its significance in worship, when Aramaic was no longer the vernacular of the Jewish communities, introduces almost insurmountable problems of dating. Even in the case of the Targum Onqelos, the date of which is very close to that of the text of the Bible, we may ask whether it reflects the beginnings of the Targum tradition or is the result of a late rabbinic normalizing of the text, when preaching and religious instruction had already been separated from the translation of the reading. Christian theologians occupied with the Targum often hope that they will find in it usable parallels to the New Testament, and therefore bring out the early features of these texts; they are followed by Jewish scholars who attempt to get back behind the rabbinic tradition. However, anyone who approaches the Targums from the rabbinic literature usually sees them as no more than the late popularization of rabbinical doctrines. In fact, in most Targums old and new are combined; they are the result of a concern lasting over a century with the abiding validity of the biblical message, testimony to a liturgical concern with the Bible, which never remained a 'dead letter' (a charge often made by Christian authors against Judaism), but was constantly appropriated anew in living dialogue with the God who speaks to Israel in the Bible.

2. Talmud and Midrash

The basic attitude sketched out above in connection with the Targum also applies in the way in which the Bible is dealt with in Talmud and Midrash, but here we see not only the result of concern with the Bible, but also constantly more explicit reflection on the right way of appropriating the Bible and its abiding significance.

As primarily a work of religious law, the earliest rabbinic text, the Mishnah, is throughout relatively independent of the Bible. Individual tractates have only a very loose connection with the Bible; granted, the theme and construction of others is given by the Bible, but the development of the theme is fairly unbiblical, and only in a few tractates do biblical quotations and their exegesis determine the structure of the text. A problem was seen here at a very early stage; one reaction to it was constantly to insert relevant biblical quotations into the text of the

Mishnah. In addition, the broader treatment of the Mishnah material in its parallel work, the Tosephta, is largely determined by an explicit reference back to the biblical foundation of the religious law, a concern which also characterizes the Talmudic commentary on the Mishnah.

The Palestinian Talmud contains relatively little material which is independently devoted to biblical exegesis in addition to the biblical commentary on the Mishnah; Palestine developed the Midrash as its own genre of literature, and devoted particular writings to the treatment of the Bible. Things were different in Babylonia. All the religious and literary concerns of the Babylonian rabbis were ultimately inserted into the framework of the Mishnah commentary. The Babylonian Talmud, that much more extensive, which soon became *the* Talmud, thus took in, among other things, major blocks of text which perhaps originally circulated as independent midrashic writings. Prominent examples are the commentary on Ex. 1–2 in the tractate Sota and that on the book of Esther in the tractate Megilla. Free from the formal conditions of an ongoing commentary on a biblical book or even on particular liturgical passages for readings, the authors or redactors of these works could work on a much wider canvas, for example incorporating into the commentary on Ex. 1–2 an extended discussion of the Samson traditions, of Gen. 37 on Judah and Tamar, sections from the Joseph story or on the death of Moses: what at first glance looks like a free collage proves on closer inspection to be determined by a view of the theology of history which sees the unity of the biblical history under the theme of promise and fulfilment, of guilt and atonement, and gives the reader perspectives for dealing in religious terms with his own history.

However, the real medium of the rabbinic concern with the Bible is and remains the Midrash, particularly as this was developed in Palestinian Judaism. The word *midrash* means 'search, explanation', especially the religious explanation of the Bible. To begin with (around the third century CE) there were Midrashim on Exodus to Deuteronomy, which were above all concerned with the legal application of these texts (they thus begin only with Ex. 12 or Num. 5, and in Deuteronomy discuss above all chs. 12–26). However, within the selected unit of texts they do not pass over the narrative and poetic passages. A Christian approach usually regards biblical regulations which no longer correspond to the legal sensibility of the time as time-conditioned, outdated statements. Jewish thought does not take such a view of the biblical statements: divine revelation can never be out of date. But as (for example) so many death penalties can no longer be inflicted by the rabbis (e.g. Deut. 21.18–21 for the rebellious son), this verse was interpreted so literally in every detail that there was practically no possibility of applying it any longer. However, no word of the Bible can be done away with: exegesis applies it to each particular situation.

In the following centuries (the fifth to the eighth) numerous commentaries were written on the Pentateuch and the scrolls: texts from the
prophets and the rest of the hagiographa were inserted into such works and
were seldom the objects of commentaries of their own (if this happened,
the commentaries were late ones). Here, too, therefore, the selection of the
texts to be commented on was largely determined by liturgical reading; in
this way the formative texts of the Bible are partly different from those in
the Christian tradition. In addition to the continuous and above all
edifying commentary on individual books, the genre of the preaching
Midrash appeared at a very early stage; this offered sermons on the
pericopes from the Pentateuch in the lectionary cycle or on the particular
sections which were readings for the festivals during the year (here there
were sometimes also sermons on the texts of the prophets). These biblical
sermons usually deal with only a very few verses of the reading, have a
more marked thematic orientation, and as illustrations often also use at
length passages from other biblical books (like Job), which otherwise play
no part.

In the late phase of the Midrash tradition (from about the eighth
century), the genre of the 'rewritten Bible', of which the period of the
Second Temple had already produced some fine examples, then crops up
again. The exegetical traditions are already so well known that, combined
with other motives, they can be used for a free retelling of the Bible in
which quotations from the text and the narrator's own statements are no
longer distinguished. Edification and entertainment is the joint aim of this
literature, which can also be a substitute for Christian or Islamic narrative
collections, from which there was a preference to keep ordinary Jewish
people away. As far as possible the Bible was to remain the sole spiritual
ground of the people of the Book.

What conceptions determine the Midrash and distinguish it from other
forms of biblical exegesis? Let us begin with a fairly external detail. In any
classical Midrash one finds different interpretations for most verses,
always quoted with the name of their author or introduced with the phrase
'another interpretation'. If even a dream can have many explanations, this
is all the more true of the Bible, as the rabbis stress: 'Any scriptural passage
has a number of meanings' (Sanhedrin 34a). There is no such thing as *the*
correct exegesis.

At the basis of this approach to the Bible is the belief that God has
revealed himself in the Bible once and for all. This revelation must
therefore apply for all times to come, for all situations in life. Any time, any
person learns from the Bible what God wills here and now. So we read in
the tractate Aboth: 'Turn and turn it (the Torah); for everything is in it.'
The text read literally is only one level; by comparison with other passages

in the Bible, careful observation of the linguistic peculiarities of the text, different forms of writing, and so on, it is possible to recognize further facets of the text which can be relevant in a particular situation. But so that a fondness for association does not lead too far from the original meaning of a word, the controlling rule is, 'The Bible does not lose its literal meaning' (Shabbat 63a).

If one understands the Bible in the fullest sense as revelation, then its linguistic form is not simply an arbitrary medium. Hebrew is the language of revelation; therefore all the linguistic aspects of the text are at the same time communications from God. So, for example, the exegete evaluates different modes of writing a word or grammatically obsolete forms as indications of a deeper meaning, and applies (popular) etymology as a means of exegesis, like the numerical value of a word (each Hebrew consonant is at the same time a number). Where the modern exegete quickly resorts to emendations and conjectures on finding incomprehensible formulations and constructions in the Bible, the rabbis in each instance attempt to cope with the text as it is and prefer to see its difficulties as indications of additional things the text means to say, or as deliberate cross-references to other passages in the Bible. Particularly in the Midrash texts of the Babylonian Talmud we often find it said of passages which still cause us textual problems today: really it should have said so and so, but the unexpected form is there to tell us something.

As an ideal form of communication the Bible is also marked by the principle of frugality: no word in it is in vain, no consonant is useless. There is no unfounded repetition in the Bible. Parallel statements in the Psalms or in other poetic texts are therefore regularly applied to different situations: where legal precepts are repeated they relate to different aspects of the law in question. 'Thou shalt not steal' in Ex. 20.16 applies to kidnapping, while 'You shall not steal' in Lev. 19.11 refers to stealing things; the thrice-repeated 'Thou shalt not seethe a kid in its mother's milk' (Ex. 23.19; 34.26; Deut. 14.21) prohibits first the cooking itself, then the enjoyment of something cooked in this way, and finally any gain from the cooking (for example in a restaurant for non-Jews). God does not repeat himself. However, so that this kind of exegesis is not taken to extremes and thus used *ad absurdum*, there is a corrective in the principle attributed to R. Ishmael: 'The Torah speaks in the language of men' (Sifre Numeri 112); in other words, it adapts itself to human peculiarities of style and manners of speaking.

The claim of the rabbis that the whole of the Bible is the word of God in all its parts, and thus is religiously significant, sometimes necessarily leads to allegorical exegesis. This is true in particular of the Song of Songs, which is not to be understood as a collection of love songs or a praise of love among human beings, but speaks of the love of God for his people Israel. It refers to the experiences of Israel, the beloved, with the beloved God of the exodus from Egypt throughout history and also already proclaims the awaited Messiah, the beloved who was so ardently hoped for by Israel.

Such an exegesis of the Song of Songs soon ceased to present any problems. It was less easy to accept the claim of religious significance for the numerous lists of names and genealogies in the Bible. What religious significance might such lists of names have? Against such objections the rabbis defended their view by saying that precisely the books of Chronicles with their numerous lists of names had been given for exegesis. It is said of R. Simon ben Pazi that he used to say in connection with the exegesis of the books of Chronicles: 'In you, all the words are the same, but we know how to expound them' (Megilla 13a). There follows a commentary on I Chron. 4.18, in which all the names are interpreted etymologically and associated with known names in the biblical history. So here we find information about Moses or about Pharaoh's daughter, who later married the spy Caleb. In this way one can get something out of mere names, and fill out one's knowledge of central figures of the Bible, seeing them as moral examples, but above all linking the events of biblical history much more closely together, so as to clarify the unity of this God-guided history all the more. Where a modern reader might make the objection that there is absolutely no historical understanding here, the rabbis reply that mere historical information has no value as long as one fails to recognize the deeper sense of history; above all, however, they stress the absolute unity of revelation: 'In the Torah there is no before and after' (Pesahim 6b).

The modern observer may regard much of this Midrash as playing with the text, and in a sense that is true. Midrash is not concerned with the deadly serious questions of scholarly exegesis; rather, it is comparable to spiritual scriptural reading, which seeks the source of the reader's own religious feeling in the Bible. In Midrash, Israel may introduce its own self with all its questions into the biblical text; in dealing with this text, the believing reader gets used to the language of revelation and personally appropriates the former liberation of Israel from Egypt, 'from a people of strange language' (Ps. 114.1) in order to have a share in the people of the Bible, to enter into dialogue with God. It can agree fully with what R. Aqiba says: '"That is no empty word which goes by you" (Deut. 32.47). But if it is empty, then that is your fault, who do not know how to interpret it' (Genesis Rabba 1.14). Midrash is to some extent God's language teaching.

3. The Middle Ages

The midrashic tradition of edifying biblical exegesis also enjoyed great popularity in the Middle Ages. But the juxtaposition of three monotheistic religions and other religious traditions increasingly brought with it the need also to provide rational proof of the correctness of one's own religion, even for outsiders. That was also particularly true of dealing with Holy Scripture, the exegesis of which was also to be possible outside the closed circle of believers. That led to a crisis for Midrash, particularly in the environment of Islam.

The Arabs regarded the linguistic perfection of the Qur'an as proof of its origin in divine revelation: the study of Arab grammar was thus as it were a theological task. Associated with this was, of course, also the quest for the literal meaning of the text to be interpreted. Within the Jewish world, from the eighth century onwards this demand was taken up above all by the Karaites, who at least in theory no longer allowed tradition as a principle of interpretation and produced a series of significant biblical exegetes.

In view of this demand, Jewish scholars, too, became increasingly concerned with the grammar of biblical language, especially as they too had the notion of a language of revelation, which for them was, of course, Hebrew. The basis was the exact fixing of the biblical text, including its vocalization and cantillation, by the Massoretes. Around the same time, Saadya Gaon (892–942) was also concerned with Hebrew grammar and a philological commentary instead of an approach to the Bible through Midrash. The simple literal meaning of the Bible now had priority. The great Jewish exegetes of North Africa and Spain also followed this model; they include Abraham Ibn Ezra from Toledo (1092–1167), in whose commentary on Deut. 1.1 some references also already indicate criticism of the Mosaic origin of the Pentateuch, criticism which Spinoza was to take up later. On his numerous travels, Ibn Ezra also established the new methods of biblical exegesis in the Judaism of Christian Europe.

But that by no means signified a direct replacement of the Midrash. The Midrash tradition also lived on in the Arab world and continued to influence commentators; it also stimulated collected works in the form of catenas. This was even more the case in Christian Europe, whose Jews were largely excluded from the cultural environment and therefore were much more bound to tradition.

In the Middle Ages, after Spain, the most significant centres of the Jewish tradition in Europe were Germany and France. Here philological commentary and a stress on the literal meaning could never manage to become completely established. Rabbi Salomo ben Isaac, called Rashi for short (1040–1105), who came from Troyes and after studying in Germany taught Bible and Talmud in his home city for many years, certainly recognized the significance of the literal meaning and was also occupied with etymological explanations; however, his heart was with the Midrash tradition, which he continually reckoned to have just as much justification. His grandson Simeon ben Meir, called Rashbam for short, in his commentary on the Pentateuch an uncompromising supporter of the simple literal sense, bears witness that Rashi in his old age increasingly turned away from a midrashic type of exegesis and intended to revise his biblical commentary. But it is precisely the fusing of new concerns with now beloved traditions which has made Rashi's biblical commentary an absolute classic. It has been disseminated in numerous manuscripts, and since the invention of printing it has been printed in all the traditional Jewish editions of the Bible. What Christian commentators in the Middle Ages knew and quoted usually comes from Rashi, who even now still provides the first approach to the Bible in traditional Jewish teaching.

Similarly influenced by the Arab environment, in the Middle Ages a philosophical approach to the Bible developed which is reminiscent of the allegorical interpretation of scripture by Philo of Alexandria. Through the writings of Moses Maimonides (1138–1205) this method also found a home in Southern France, where the Jewish communities had close contacts with the Islamic world; here above all David Kimchi, Levi ben Gershom and Joseph Ibn Kaspi attempted to ground philosophical teachings in the Bible.

Mystical exegesis of the Bible, which was similarly concerned with the deeper sense of the text, was often associated with philosophical allegory. Moses ben Nachman (1195–1270) already keeps referring in connection with the literal sense of a passage to the secret sense; the Kabbala then develops this approach particularly. Its main work, the Zohar (late thirteenth century), which has the form of a commentary on the Pentateuch, the Song of Songs and Ruth, combines midrashic traditions with the simple literal sense and mystical interpretations.

The Zohar also contains for the first time in Jewish literature an explicit statement of the doctrine of the fourfold meaning of scripture, summed up in the word *pardes*, 'paradise', in connection with the Talmudic narrative of the four rabbis who ascended to Paradise. The consonants of the word denote the simple literal meaning (*peshat*), the allegorical meaning (*remez* = 'reference'), edifying midrashic exegesis (*derash*) and finally the mystical sense (*sod* = 'mystery'). With the dissemination of the Zohar and its approach to the Bible this fourfold exegesis with special stress on the mystical sense long enjoyed great popularity.

Belief in the divine revelation of the Bible and the consciousness of having in the Bible the primal document of their own existence has for a long time, indeed in part to the present, kept alive among the people of the book a traditional approach to Holy Scripture to which the questions and problems of modern critical biblical scholarship must remain alien.

Translated by John Bowden

Readers of Scripture and Hearers of the Word in the Mediaeval Church

Pim Valkenberg

A twentieth-century tourist who looks at the remains of mediaeval culture in Western Europe might well be inclined to think that the Christian religion, and therefore also the Bible, exercised an all-important influence at this time. Biblical concepts stand out clearly in the sculpture, music, manuscripts and legends of the time. The Bible was read, sung, illustrated and copied in the Middle Ages.

However, this is only part of the truth: the image that we have of the Middle Ages is governed by the products of a small, literate upper class in mediaeval society. Since the educational system of Christian Western Europe was in the hands of the church, the clergy had a monopoly in the sphere of scholarship and letters (in Latin).[1] So it is possible to present a picture of the way in which the clergy read the Bible in the Middle Ages, but it is far more difficult to discover how the great majority of the illiterate heard, saw and understood the Bible in the mediaeval churches.

This problem determines the structure of this article. It is limited to the twelfth and thirteenth centuries, because these are generally seen as the most interesting and most fruitful period for mediaeval exegesis.[2] In the first part I shall look at the way in which the monks and theologians read the Bible, and in the second part I shall seek an answer to the question how the Bible was heard by those who could not read it or were not in a position to do so.

The monastic reading of scripture

In his classic work on monastic spirituality in the Middle Ages J. Leclercq corrects a widespread view of theology in the twelfth century: it did not involve just a number of forerunners of the scholasticism which blossomed in the thirteenth century, but above all also formed the climax of a monastic theology which is a continuation of patristic theology.[3] In this monastic theology, scripture along with its exposition by the church fathers is the obvious starting point. From the ninth to the twelfth century the majority of commentaries on scripture were written by monks: in their exegesis they paid a good deal of attention to the actual words of scripture, which was treated with great respect. Monastic reading and exegesis of scripture is focussed on the monks' own world: they sought to give expression to a way of life which was focussed on a desire for the God of whom a foretaste could already be acquired in this life. Moreover the reading of scripture was also at the service of meditation, in which scripture was appropriated as it were by ruminating on it.[4] Attention to the spiritual needs of the monastic community also determined the way in which scripture was appropriated – in other words the hermeneutical process. Scripture was read as an expression of the same desire for God, and as a testimony to the salvation history in which God constantly seeks to make himself known through human beings. Whereas the salvation-historical line was worked out in the twelfth century above all by some Benedictines like Rupert of Deutz (1070–1130), the appropriation of salvation by the monastic soul was central for the Cistercians, of whom Bernard of Clairvaux (1090–1163) was the prime example.[5] Bernard's commentary in the form of preaching is the aptest form of expression of this affective theology in which the experience of union with God is central.

The importance of scripture in the monastic life of prayer can be traced in language: those who sing, listen to and read scripture so often themselves begin to speak in the language of scripture without any longer being aware of the fact. Theological language then becomes a mosaic of allusions and stylistic references to scripture. In this respect Bernard continues the tradition of Augustine.[6]

An intermediate form; the regular canons of Saint Victor

It is possible to point to different schools in twelfth-century theology and scriptural exegesis.[7] On the one hand there are schools which are associated with the monasteries; on the other hand schools start coming into being in the cities which develop into new intellectual centres. It is this latter type of school which gave its name to scholastic theology: here attention was paid to scientific questioning as a way of handing down the faith through instruction. In his *Sic et non*, Peter Abelard (1079–1142) coined methodological doubt as a way of making apparently contradictory statements of the church fathers agree.[8]

Moreover there were contacts between the two types of school: while the Benedictine Anselm of Canterbury (1033–1109) was leading the monastic school of Bec, at the same time he developed the classical-scholastic programme of faith in search of understanding (*fides quaerens intellectum*) with the help of reason. On the other hand Anselm of Laon (1050–1117) led a city school the aim of which was to gloss the whole of scripture by means of patristic texts; it is to this group that we owe the *glossa ordinaria* which for centuries was an indispensable help in the exegesis of scripture.[9] The same concern for maintaining the patristic heritage led to the production of systematic collections, of which Peter Lombard's *Sentences* (1095–1160) had the most influence.

Monastic and scholastic theology thus do not form two separate worlds, though they do exist in different socio-cultural contexts: the relatively closed character of culture within the monastery contrasts with the openness to the great variety of city life in the new schools. In this respect the canons who lived according to the Augustine rule in the monastery of Saint Victor in Paris occupied a distinctive position: they tried to combine the advantages of the monastery with those of the city school.[10] The central place of scripture in their study programme emerges clearly in the works of Hugo of Saint Victor (1096–1141), and his nickname 'the second Augustine' clearly hints at this: it is a renewal of the programme that Augustine developed in *De doctrina christiana*. In his *Didascalicon* Hugh discusses the profane sciences as the means for the study of scripture in its literal sense. The allegorical significance of scripture arises in second place: in this connection, in *De sacramentis Christianae fidei* Hugo develops a synthesis of the doctrine of faith in the perspective of salvation history. Finally follows the tropological meaning of scripture, which is orientated on the virtues. According to this programme every student had to read through the whole of scripture several times in order to discover constantly deeper meanings in it.[11]

Beryl Smalley has pointed out that a tendency becomes evident in the school of Saint Victor towards a more rational and critical exegesis of scripture: the literal sense of scripture must come first, even if this does not accord with the traditional Christian exegesis. For a trustworthy exegesis of prophetic texts like Isaiah 7.14, Andrew of St Victor (died 1175) often turns to Jewish exegesis.[12]

The scholastic reading of scripture

It is misleading to see the contributions of the scholastic readers of scripture all along the same line: just as in the twelfth and thirteenth centuries the Platonic picture of the world was gradually replaced by the philosophy of Aristotle, in whom the empirical knowledge of earthly reality occupies a greater place, so the contemplative reading of scripture which draws attention to its spiritual meaning gradually gave place to a more rational reading of scripture which takes only the literal meaning as the starting point for scientific questions. Such a crude sketch of the rise of scholasticism and the way in which it dealt with scripture is not unfounded, but it suffers from a rationalistic prejudice:[13] even in its renewed scientific procedure, scholasticism remained faithful to the way in which the church fathers read scripture. Whereas the typical technique of questioning (*quaestio*) develops from the reading of the text (*lectio*), scripture still remains the background to the theological *quaestio*. Moreover, the usual title for an independent theologian in the thirteenth century is *Magister in sacra Pagina*: he reads scripture with his pupils, discusses with them the problems that arise, and proclaims scripture in the academic community.[14]

In the meantime the university as a new context for reading scripture seems to have provided a number of innovations. Not only does the number of biblical manuscripts increase explosively in the new thirteenth-century milieu, but a number of new aids for studying scripture come into being. Thus a semi-official standard text of the Vulgate was established by the University of Paris on the basis of the division into chapters made by Stephen Langton (1150–1228).[15] At the same time, around 1235, the first concordance of the Vulgate was made in the Dominican convent of St Jacques in Paris, a work in which Hugo de Saint-Cher (1195-1263) was involved.[16] Both Stephen and Hugo yet again provided the whole of scripture with a commentary. In this way the conditions were created for a scientifically responsible study of scripture at a time when this was still dominated by Jerome's Latin text.

Thomas Aquinas as a model

In general, scholastic theology was not directly associated with the study of scripture. It is therefore important to see what the role of scripture is in the theology of Thomas Aquinas (1225–1274), since he is generally regarded as the most important theologian of the scholastic period. As a Dominican and theologian in Paris (1252–1259; 1269–1272), did he profit from the favourable conditions for the scholarly study of scripture there? I shall present some arguments which suggest that this may have been the case.

The importance of scripture for Thomas becomes clear at a theoretical level in the texts which he devotes to the question what theology really is. In these texts Thomas seems to sense to an increasing degree that theology is a science by being based on God's revelation as the principle from which it begins.[17] In this connection Thomas uses the term 'instruction in faith' (*sacra doctrina*), something to which both scripture and theology belong: theology is part of a process of instruction in the faith that the theologian receives from God by means of scripture, and that he himself in turn hands on to his pupils in theological instruction. This means that scripture is not only the most important source used in theological argumentation but is also the source and framework of this argumentation itself. Because scripture is not just used in theology but is first of all received, theology is a scientific form of scripture-reading within the sphere of faith in which scripture is interpreted in the best possible way, with all the relevant disciplines, in order to do justice to what God has to say for the people of each new time.

Now if Thomas's theological practice is to correspond with this theoretical description, scripture must not only be the most important authority in his argumentation – that can be demonstrated purely in statistical terms – but the argumentation as such must also be developed with an eye to the exegesis of scripture.

In other words, any theological *quaestio* has to be a question about scripture (*quaestio in Sacro Pagina*).

In this connection it is worth noting that a number of differences between Thomas's first work of systematic theology (his *Scriptum super Sententiis*, a commentary on the *Sentences* of Peter Lombard) and his last work of systematic theology (the *Summa theologiae*) can best be explained by a reference to his professional work as a commentator on scripture, which lasted over many years. Here I shall give two instances which are derived from Thomas's theology of the resurrection of Christ.[18]

Whereas in his *Sentences* Peter Lombard discusses the resurrection of Christ only in an eschatological context (Book IV), Thomas in his commentary on the christological part of Book III adds a question about the resurrection of Christ. However, he discusses the saving significance of the resurrection of Christ for our resurrection in the general eschatology of Book IV of his commentary. In his *Summa theologiae*, by contrast, Thomas already discusses the resurrection of Christ in his christology. This theme has not only become more important in the *Summa* than it was in the *Scriptum*, but has been given another place. This shift can be explained by the influence of a text of Paul, 'Jesus who was delivered over for our misdeeds and raised for our justification' (cf. Rom. 4.25). Paul compelled Thomas as it were to adapt his theological system:[19] if the resurrection of Christ has an influence on the sacramental life of Christians under grace (cf. Rom. 6.4.11), then this theme can no longer be discussed only in an eschatological context. The fact that Thomas wrote a second commentary on Romans in the years preceding the christology of his *Summa* also provides an explanation of this remarkable shift.

The second example involves apparently only a small detail. In his *Scriptum* Thomas asks whether Christ had to prove his resurrection to the disciples with arguments. The background to this question is shaped by the word *argumenta* in the Vulgate of Acts 1.3: 'After his death he showed them that he was alive with many proofs.' In his answer Thomas sees a connection between Christ who proves his resurrection with arguments and the theologian who proves the principles of faith with arguments.[20] Whereas the question in the *Scriptum* is influenced by earlier works of systematic theology,[21] in his *Summa* Thomas goes to work more independently. Here he again discusses the significance of *argumentum* in Acts 1.3, but this time he describes the activity of Christ as 'making manifest' (*manifestare* as a synonym of *revelare*) in place of 'proving' (*probare*). An analysis shows that he arrives at this change on the basis of three insights: 1. (*academic theoretical insight*) In matters of faith which we know from God's revelation, arguments do not form strict proofs which make faith adhere to something that was doubtful, but they are visible signs which show the truth of something else; 2. (*theological insight*) God does not compel people to faith but leaves their freedom intact; 3. (*exegetical insight*) *tekmeria* in Acts 1.3 means 'signs' in place of 'arguments'.[22]

This illustration makes it clear how Thomas later corrects his initial comparison between the scientific argumentation of the scholastic and the way in which Christ deals with his disciples, under the influence of a better insight into the text of scripture.

These two illustrations, inadequate though they are, make it clear that there is a development in Thomas's theology. Under the influence of his scripture commentaries and the insight that theology is dependent on God's revelation, Thomas's theology comes to be more concentrated on the essential. This implies that scripture, along with the church fathers as interpreters of scripture, not only occupies a statistically greater place in Thomas's *Summa* than in his earlier works, but in so doing comes more clearly to the fore as the source and framework of theology itself: the questions in the *Summa* relate to scripture directly or indirectly, and the answers to these questions are given in the framework of the transmission of faith which is always at the same time the reading of scripture. In this respect Thomas's theology is 'biblical theology'.[23] The supporting scriptural quotations with which Thomas often concludes his arguments are, moreover, simply a reference to the scripture which is already being investigated from the beginning of the train of thought. This too is a literary form which Thomas takes over from his biblical commentaries; the exegesis of scripture is further confirmed by the word of scripture itself.

The mendicant orders and the model of the New Testament

In a balanced conclusion the editors of an imposing collection of studies of the Bible in the Middle Ages have pointed out that in the twelfth century a change took place in the way in which the Bible was understood: from the Carolingian Renaissance (c.800) to the investiture dispute (c.1100), church and society were dominated by models primarily drawn from the Old Testament; by contrast, in the twelfth century a new model appears: apostolic life in the steps of Jesus and his disciples.[24] This ideal of a *vita apostolica* plays a major role in the rise of the mendicant orders, but it is alive in wider circles. The Waldensians are a clear instance of this new ideal.[25] After the rich merchant Valdes was gripped by the gospel around 1175, he and his followers followed the gospel literally: they began to travel round preaching and disseminating the gospel in the vernacular; they lived in community and obtained the wherewithal to live on by begging and selling their translations of the Bible. Although the ideal of evangelical poverty could count on the approval of the church, and the church authorities were not in principle hostile to translations of the Bible into the vernacular, the Waldensian movement was eventually expelled from the church because its members wanted to keep preaching by laity, quite apart from the local clergy. The same ideal led to the rise of the mendicant orders, which were at least in part an attempt to make the new biblical verve which had been experienced by Waldensians and partly also by Albigensians bear fruit within the church. This is evident from the life-story of St Dominic (1170–1221), the founder of the order of preaching brothers. Moreover the same characteristics can already be found among the new mendicant orders which already began to determine the pastoral and theological face of the church in the thirteenth century: proximity to the new class of citizens in the cities, evangelical poverty, an itinerant life of preaching, and emphasis on the study of scripture. It is notable that in the thirteenth century the Franciscans and Dominicans soon already formed the majority of theologians who were commenting on scripture, and that they also had a hand in disseminating the Bible in Latin and in the vernacular.[26]

This passion for the apostolic life led to the mendicant orders developing a new hermeneutic in which discipleship of Christ according to the letter of the gospel came to occupy a central place. Thus for example Panella[27] thinks that Thomas Aquinas developed a new hermeneutic in his scripture commentaries and in his polemical works in which the person of Christ and the gospel come to have a central position as a 'new law'. Just as the monks in the twelfth century appropriated scripture with a view to their life of prayer, so the mendicant orders in the thirteenth century adopted scripture with a view to their practical discipleship of Christ in a life of poverty and preaching.

However, the way in which scripture was used differed, depending on the literary genre and the purpose of the author. Wheras in the systematic theological works of Thomas Aquinas there is seldom if ever any mention of an identification between the life of the mendicant orders and the apostolic life of the disciples of Christ, there clearly is this identification in his polemical works and sometimes in his scripture commentaries and sermons. This means that the attitude of the theologian who in his exegesis of scripture is trying to do justice to the word of God is different from the attitude of the theologian who is trying to convince his colleagues. In this last case we have an identification in which part of scripture is stressed, whereas silence is kept about other parts. Precisely because of the importance of scripture in the Middle Ages, this phenomenon often appears: in the polemic over the church reforms of Pope Gregory VII and the investiture controversy; in the discussions between Waldensians and Cathari; in the dispute over evangelical poverty among the Franciscans; and in the dispute between the mendicant orders and the secular clergy in the University of Paris.[28]

Hearers of the word

As I mentioned right at the beginning of this article, for a survey of the importance of scripture in the Middle Ages it is not enough just to discuss scripture as read; the vast majority of the population was illiterate, and thus could get to know scripture only through what they heard and saw of it. Alongside art and the lives of the saints, [29] preaching was the most important means of making scripture accessible to broad strata of the population. In this preaching a literate upper stratum of the population, merchants like Valdes and Francis of Assisi, became intermediaries after their conversion: a preaching movement came into being for and by lay people in the vernacular, which determined the conflicts between the Waldensians, and also the mendicant orders, and the church authorities.[30] This conflict stresses the importance of preaching as handing on the word of God.

The sermons which have come down from the thirteenth century, in Latin or in the vernacular, show considerable diversity.[31] So I shall again restrict to myself to the university milieu of Paris which helped to bring to birth a large number of books of sermons which were used by the mendicant orders. D'Avray[32] has put forward the hypothesis that Paris was the centre of the dissemination of sermons in the thirteenth century, not least because it was the centre of scholasticism: scholastic scripture-reading seems to have been a good seedbed for model sermons.

On closer investigation it is striking that there is a great similarity between the scripture commentaries of these theologians and their sermons: the content of the written text is divided up and analysed in a painstaking way; the analysis is then further illuminated with other quotations from scripture, many of which are taken from a concordance. Moreover, the tone of the argument is more personal than in systematic theological works by the same author.[33] Scholastic scripture-reading determined the way in which sermons were often delivered, namely as a collection of texts with biblical quotations to illustrate them. The preacher could fill in this framework according to the circumstances. Here he often used *exempla*, stories and images to make concrete the biblical text being used. [34]

The use of these stories and images, which were also handed on in separate collections, gives us some insight into the way in which the audience got to hear the word: whereas in the Latin academic sermons for a literate public the doctrine of faith was developed in abstract terms, in sermons for an illiterate audience this same doctrine of faith was made vivid in images and stories. In this way a connection was introduced between the word of scripture and daily life.

Another way of bringing illiterate people into contact with the word of scripture was catechesis. This often happened in the form of catechetical sermons, like for example the series of sermons on the Creed, the Ten Commandments, the Lord's Prayer and the Hail Mary which Thomas Aquinas gave in the vernacular at Naples during Lent 1273. In addition to the abundant use of scripture, it is striking that these sermons are divided into two: first the doctrine of faith is developed, and then the consequences for morality are discussed. In this way there is a connection between piety and conduct. According to Leclercq,[35] the life of prayer and moral conduct are the two aspects which determined the 'question' of the illiterate and literate laity alike; the mendicant orders tried to respond to this question with their 'offer' of scripture, translated into and preached in the vernacular.

Translated by John Bowden

Notes

1. Cf. R. W. Southern, *Western Society and the Church in the Middle Ages*, The Pelican History of the Church 2, Harmondsworth 1970, 38; M. Richter, 'Latina lingua – sacra seu vulgaris', in W. Lourdaux and D. Verhelst (ed.), *The Bible and Medieval Culture*, Mediaevalia Lovaniensia, Series I studia 7, Louvain 1979, 16.

2. C. Spicq, *Esquisse d'une histoire de l'exégèse latine au Moyen Age*, Bibliothèque Thomiste 26, Paris 1944, 7; B. Smalley, *The Bible in the Middle Ages*, Oxford ³1983, 347–60; id., 'The Bible in the Mediaeval Schools', in G. W. H. Lampe (ed.), *The Cambridge History of the Bible II: The West from the Fathers to the Reformation*, Cambridge 1969, 204–7.

3. Dom J.Leclercq, *L'amour des lettres et le désir de Dieu: initiation aux auteurs monastiques du Moyen Age*, Paris 1957, 9–11, 179–218.

4. Leclercq, *Amour des lettres* (n.3), 70–88; cf. J. Dubois, 'Comment les moines du Moyen Age chantaient et goûtaient les Saintes Ecritures', in P. Riché and G. Lobrichon (eds.), *Le Moyen Age et la Bible*, Bible de tous les temps 4, Paris 1984, 261–98.

5. Leclercq, *Amour des lettres* (n.3), 208.

6. Cf. J. Longère, 'La prédication en langue latin', in Riché and Lobrichon, *Moyen Age* (n.4), 527–9; A.-M. la Bonnardière (ed.), *Saint Augustin et la Bible*, Bible de tous les temps 3, Paris 1986.

7. Cf.J. Chatillon, 'La Bible dans les écoles du XIIe siècle', in Riché and Lobrichon, *Moyen Age* (n.4), 163–97.

8. Peter Abelard, prologue to *Sic et Non* (ed. Boyer and McKeon, Chicago and London 1976, 103); cf. L. M. de Rijk, *Middeleeuwse wijsbegeerte*, Assen and Amsterdam 1977, 124.

9. Cf. G. Lobrichon, 'Une nouveauté: les gloses de la Bible', in Riché and Lobrichon, *Moyen Age* (n.4), 95–114; B. Smalley, 'Glossa ordinaria', in *Theologische Realenzyklopädie* XIII, Berlin 1984, 452–7.

10. Smalley, *Bible in the Middle Ages* (n.2), 83.

11. Ibid., 89; H. de Lubac, *Exégèse Médiévale* II/1, Paris 1961.

12. Smalley, *Bible in the Middle Ages* (n.2), 149–85.

13. H. de Lubac, *Exégèse Médiévale* I, Paris 1959, 13.

14. M.–D. Chenu, *La théologie comme science au XIIIᵉ siècle*, Bibliothèque Thomiste 33, Paris ³1957, 21–5.

15. R. Loewe, 'The Medieval History of the Latin Vulgate', in Lampe, *Cambridge History of the Bible* II (n.2), 145–8.

16. M. A. and R. H. Rouse, 'La concordance verbale des Écritures', in Riché and Lobrichon, *Moyen Age* (n.4), 116.

17. See especially the first *quaestio* of the *Summa theologiae*; cf. the analysis by M. Cobrin, *Le Chemin de la théologie chez Thomas d'Aquin*, Bibliothèque des Archives de Philosophie, nouvelle série 16, Paris 1974.

18. See *Scriptum super III Sententiarum* d.21 q.2 and *Scriptum super IV Sententiarum* d.43 a.2, and *Summa Theologiae* III, qq.53–6.

19. See S. Lyonnet, 'La valeur sotériologique de la résurrection du Christ selon saint Paul', *Gregorianum* 39, 1958, 295–318; T. Schoof, 'Jezus, Gods werktuig voor ons heil. Peiling naar de theologische procedure van Thomas van Aquino', *Tijdschrift voor Theologie* 14, 1974, 217–44.

20. Cf. *Scriptum super III Sententiarum* d.21 with *Scriptum super I Sententiarum* prol. a.5.

21. Namely the *Summa aurea* of William of Auxerre (Lib. IV tract. 18. cap 2) and the *Summa fratris Alexandri* (Lib. III tract. 6 q.2 tit.2).

22. See *Summa theologiae* III q.55 n.5.

23. M–D. Chenu, *Introduction à l'étude de Saint Thomas d'Aquin*, Montreal and Paris 1950, 22.

24. Riché and G. Lobrichon (eds.), *Moyen Age* (n.4), 615–18.

25. Cf. R. E. Lerner, 'Les communautés hérétiques (1150–1500)', in Riché and Lobrichon (eds.), *Moyen Age* (n.4), 597–606.

26. Cf. J. Verger, 'L'exégèse de l'Université', in Riché and Lobrichon (eds.), *Moyen Age* (n.4), 203; C. L. Sneddon, 'The "Bible du XIIIe siècle". Its Medieval Public in the light of its Manuscript Tradition', in Lourdaux and Verhelst (eds.), *Bible and Medieval Culture* (n.1), 137–40.

27. E. Panella, 'La "Lex nova" tra storia ed ermeneutica. Le occasioni dell' esegesi di S. Tommaso d'Aquino', *Memorie Domenicane* 6, 1975, 11–106.

28. See J. Leclercq, 'Usage et abus de la Bible au temps de la réforme grégorienne', in Lourdaux and Verhelst, *Bible and Medieval Culture* (n.1), 89–108; C. Thouzellier, 'L'emploi de la Bible par les cathares (XIIIe S)', ibid., 141–56; R. Manselli, 'L'apocalisse e l'interpretazione francescana della storia', ibid., 157–70; P. Riché, 'La Bible et la vie politique dans le haut Moyen Age', in Riché and Lobrichon (eds.), *Moyen Age* (n.4), 385–400; B. Smalley, 'Use of the "Spiritual" Sense of Scripture in Persuasion and Argument by Scholars of the Middle Ages', *Recherches de Théologie Ancienne et Médiévale* 52, 1985, 44–63.

29. See F. Garnier, 'L'imagerie biblique médiévale', in Riché and Lobrichon (eds.), *Moyen Age* (n.4), 401–28; M.van Uytfanghe, 'Modèles bibliques dans l'hagiographie', ibid., 449–88.

30. Cf. R. Zerfass, *Der Streit um die Laienpredigt: eine pastoralgeschichtliche Untersuchung zum Verständnis des Predigtamtes und zu seiner Entwicklung im 12. und 13.Jahrhundert*, Freiburg, Basle and Vienna 1974.

31. See M. Zink, 'La prédiction en langues vernaculaires', in Riché and Lobrichon, *Moyen Age* (n.4), 489–516; J. Longère, 'La prediction en langue latine', ibid., 517–36.

32. D. L. D'Avray, *The Preaching of the Friars: Sermons Diffused from Paris before 1300*, Oxford 1985.

33. For Thomas Aquinas see J. P. Torrell, 'La pratique pastorale d'un théologien du XIIIe siècle; Thomas d'Aquin prédicateur', *Revue Thomiste* 82, 1982, 213–45; B. Smalley, *The Gospels in the Schools*, London 1985, 257–71.

34. C. Bremond, J. le Goff and J. –C. Schmitt, '*L'exemplum*', Typologie des sources 40, Turnhout 1982; L. J. Bataillon, '*Similitudines* et *Exempla* dans les sermons du XIIIe siècle', in K. Walsh and D. Wood (eds.), *The Bible in the Mediaeval World*, Oxford 1985, 191–205.

35. J.Leclercq, 'Les traductions de la Bible et la spiritualité médiévale', in Lourdaux and Verhelst (eds.), *Bible and Medieval Culture* (n.1), 263–77.

The Sixteenth-Century Reformers and the Bible

Cornelis Augustijn

In the dedication of the first edition of his New Testament, Erasmus sings the praises of the 'evangelical and apostolic books'. In them is revealed the word of heaven which has come to us from the heart of the Father, 'more powerfully and impressively than anywhere else'.[1] I deliberately begin with these words, not only because they indicate precisely what was the deepest cause of the concern of the sixteenth-century Protestants with the Bible, but also because they come from someone who was not among the Reformers. The Reformation brought new things, but it was not a *creatio ex nihilo*. It stood in a broad stream which among other things was characterized by a new enthusiasm for the Bible and a keen curiosity about the Bible, about the languages in which it was written and the message which it brought.[2] For people of that time these facets belong together. Hebrew was the language in which God himself had spoken to the patriarchs. In those terms, at any rate, Reuchlin defended his interest in the language and the book of the Jews.[3] On the eve of the Reformation it was the common conviction of a cultured upper class that through these texts we primarily come into contact with Christ, and indeed with God. Only against this background can we form a good picture of what the Reformers did with the Bible. So in what follows the Protestants stand at the centre, but this does not at any point represent an opposition to the old church. It will be necessary at times to point out the differences between the Lutheran tradition and the Reformed tradition deriving from Zwingli and Calvin. However, in the area with which this article is concerned the agreements between the two traditions are very much greater than the differences.

I begin by asserting that the Reformation and the Bible belong together.

That comes very close to an old-fashioned Protestant apologia which follows simple lines: Catholicism means 'church' and 'sacrament', Protestantism means 'Bible', though of course we cannot put it quite like that.

The reality is slightly different. The late Middle Ages show an intense need for contact with God. The piety of this time is characterized by this need. However, the answer given by church and theology was disappointing; it lacked impulses for renewal and simply pressed towards an intensification of the usual means: more masses, more pilgrimages, more veneration of the saints, more devotion to Mary, more penitence. So the accent came to lie increasingly strongly on the intermediary authorities, on all that existed as a bridge between God and human beings.[4]

However, many people felt that what was meant to be a bridge was more of a barrier. To a large extent the Reformation must primarily be understood as the question of a direct, immediate and personal contact with God. In this respect the Protestant Reformation and the Catholic reform movement are one. Moreover Reformation and Bible belong together in the sense that the Bible *par excellence* satisfied this quest for a direct contact with God. In the Heidelberg Catechism of 1563, one of the classic confessional writings of Reformed Protestantism, we find this trait expressed in a model way. The question whether images could be accepted in the church as 'books of the laity' was answered like this: 'No, for we must not seek to be wiser than God, who does not want his Christians to be instructed by dumb images but by the living proclamation of his word.'[5] But the argument was no more regarded as conclusive than it was in the time of Gregory the Great. That becomes clear through major groups in the sixteenth century, and not just within Reformed Protestantism.

In the sixteenth century the Bible, the word of God and the gospel were usurped by the Protestants. I shall give just one example from the first period, when the term 'Protestants' was not yet being used for the supporters of the new movement. The soldiers who accompanied the Elector John of Saxony and Landgrave Philip of Hessen to the Reichstag of Spiers in 1526 had as the inscription on the backs of their cloaks, *Verbum dei manet in aeternum*, 'The Word of God abides for ever' (Isa. 40.8 = I Peter 1.25), and that was meant as a declaration of the principles of the Reformation.[6] At the beginning of the 1520s the word 'gospel' had even become fashionable; it served as a slogan under which were brought together all the aspirations of the supporters of Luther and Zwingli. This stress on the 'word of God' or 'gospel' had a polemical focus. The term expressed the need to leave aside all the additional, accumulated tradition and to return to the first beginnings, when all was still pure and unmixed. At the same time this original content was derived from God as the source, so that the term was also the expression of a proud self-awareness.[7]

This high esteem for the Bible was expressed in three ways.

First, mention needs to be made of the translations of the Bible.[8] In themselves, of course, they are not a typically Protestant phenomenon, but in the sixteenth century, when a large number of new translations appeared, the vast majority of them were of Protestant origin. They begin with Luther's translation of the New Testament in 1522 and of the Old Testament in sections, until the translation of the Bible was complete in 1534. In a later phase it became the communal work of the Wittenberg theologians, who regularly met as a translation committee. The aim was set high: Luther wanted to make the Holy Spirit speak in German, so the translation had to be one of dynamic equivalence. It was made from the Greek and Hebrew, and also included the apocryphal (deutero-canonical) books. In Germany it became *the* translation. The best evidence for this is provided by the rival 'Catholic' translations of Emser and Dietenberger (1527, 1534), which in fact differ from Luther's translation only very slightly. Luther's translation also served as a model elsewhere. Switzerland got the Zurich Bible (1531) and England the Tyndale Bible, the first part of which, the New Testament, was published in Worms in 1526. In the Netherlands, partial translations under the influence of Luther's German and Erasmus' Latin translation appeared as early as 1523, and in 1526 the first complete translation of the Bible, derived from Luther where his translation was ready and otherwise translated from the Vulgate. The Catholic production of translations from the Vulgate came about only at a late stage, and these never attained the status of the Protestant translations.

Above all in Reformed Protestantism this status was high. In the initial period that emerges, for example, in the Netherlands in the interrogation of prisoners suspected of heresy. They are always asked whether they own Bibles and this is rarely denied.[9] It was known of the Baptists that they had 'tasted' the Bible.[10] The arrangement of a Reformed church building is very telling. At the optical centre stands the pulpit with the Bible lying open on it, from which the 'preacher' or 'minister of the word' – in all languages the name for the clergy – delivers (i.e. reads out and expounds) God's word.[11] Although the parallel with altar and tabernacle is inaccurate in terms of liturgical history, it is obvious. At the same time the shift in the concept of ministry is evident. The primary task of the Protestant clergy is to expound God's word. They remain the mediators of salvation, but this is a salvation that comes to human beings not in sacramental actions but in sermons. So they also become scholars, whose robe of office is the toga, and who are depicted on tombstones with a Bible rather than a chalice in their hands.

However, the liturgical use of the translation was not the most important thing. Central was the conviction that only the word of God brings the believer into contact with God, and that conversely anyone can come into contact with God through the Bible without the mediation of human beings or things. Moreover, the ideal is that everyone should read the Bible every day. Here too this is not exclusively a matter for Protestants, nor is it typically Protestant. At a later period household prayers developed, in which the head of the household read and expounded to the members of the family a passage from the Bible morning and evening. This custom arose among the English Puritans and was then taken over on the continent.[12]

Secondly comes the question of the way in which the Bible functioned in theology among the Reformers. As well as being city preacher in Wittenberg, Luther was also associated with the still-new university as professor of biblical studies, and fulfilled both functions all his life. He did this work with heart and soul, as is evident from the fact that immediately after the appearance of Erasmus' New Testament in 1516 he incorporated its text and notes into his lectures, and in 1518 brought the young Greek scholar Melanchthon to Wittenberg to raise the level of teaching.[13] In the Reformation tradition biblical exegesis became the nucleus of theology; indeed it has to be said that the two coincided for decades. Even the first dogmatic handbook, Melanchthon's *Loci communes* ('Main concepts'), simply set out to discuss a number of key biblical concepts without making any systematic connection between them.[14] In exegesis the rhetorical method which had been developed by the humanists was adopted by the younger scholars. Specifically this meant that the influence of the *Glossa ordinaria*, with its minimal concern for philological exegesis and its embedding of the biblical text in the patristic tradition, was displaced in favour of the philological approach.[15] Of course the differences between the Reformers remain marked. In 1532 Melanchthon gave an exegesis of the Letter to the Romans in which he treated it as a tractate constructed on the rhetorical method.[16] By contrast, in the last years of his life Luther discussed Genesis and in ten years – and 2200 pages in the modern edition – barely got through it.[17] It is not surprising that purely philological work did not take up the major part of this treatment.

But there was an important point of unity among the Lutheran biblical exegetes. The central biblical notion of the whole of the Lutheran tradition was the justification of the sinner by grace, without any human merits or works. This hermeneutical centre can be seen everywhere. In Luther's translation of the Bible, Romans 3.28 read 'Man is justified through faith alone', and Luther defended this tendentious translation with verve – and moreover with good arguments.[18] In the lectures on Genesis which I have already mentioned, Cain becomes the model of those who seek to justify themselves and Abel is the model of those who live by faith.[19] Luther's followers adopted precisely the same approach.

In the Reformed tradition the accent was also on the exposition of the Bible, and although here the stress on justification by faith alone was less exclusive, here too Paul formed the centre of the Bible.[20] These exegetical works were a good means of propaganda in Catholic areas. Thus in 1529 the Strasbourg reformer Martin Bucer published a pseudonymous commentary on the Psalms which in all kinds of details suggested a French origin and was specially intended for the French market.[21] Someone who used it in remote Friesland was so enthusiastic about it – and at the same time so unrealistic – that he wrote to Bucer that he alone could sell 200 copies there.[22] The criticism expressed by Calvin, that Bucer here was obscuring justification by faith,[23] overlooks the fact that elements of Paul are also smuggled into the commentary.

Zurich, the cradle of Reformed Protestantism, had no university. So Zwingli himself formed an institute, the so-called 'prophecy'.[24] Here, several times a week, a portion of the Bible was first studied and discussed by the clergy of the city in the original language; after that the passage from the Bible was expounded in the form of a sermon to the community. It is interesting that the laity, too, were involved. The same thing happened in Geneva, though there, too, these practices were primarily intended for the preachers. The Dutch Reformed refugees who had formed their own community in London at the time of Edward VI and Elizabeth I were also familiar with 'prophecy', but there it was explicitly meant for members of the community.[25] We can see how markedly Reformed Protestantism was focussed on theological instruction. The ideal was clearly that the community should consist of people who knew what they believed and who in the first place knew their Bible. When Geneva got a university in 1559, that of course meant first of all a theological training. Here, too, the exposition of the Bible was central. Lectures have been preserved which were given by Beza, Calvin's successor, that show a structure which corresponds to this starting point. First of all Beza expounded the text philologically, then came the consequences in the sphere of systematic theology and finally the use that could be made of the text in polemic with Catholics and other opponents.[26] With this method Beza stands at the beginning of the transition to the independence of systematic and apologetic theology which was achieved at the end of the century.

A third factor is the most important: reading the Bible and preaching in the liturgy. It is the most important because in a Protestant community of faith the Bible functions most directly in Bible reading and preaching, and because these two elements form the heart of the church service. It is beyond question that preaching in the reform movements of the late Middle Ages had already taken on a distinct status of its own. That is true to the same degree of the mendicant orders, the *Devotio moderna*, the observant movement and the reform movement of Meaux,[27] however much they may have differed from one another. But there remains a difference in principle over the position which preaching took on in the Reformation. However important preaching may have been, in any late mediaeval movement the celebration of the eucharist remained the heart of worship, and the proclamation of the word which preceded it had a propaedeutic character.

In the Reformation tradition this changes. Luther felt himself primarily to be a preacher, and not without reason; on average he preached in the city church of Wittenberg twice or three times a week. On Sundays he kept to the pericope system of the old church, although he was not very successful in so doing. However, he thought that the annual repetition was worthwhile for simple people and equally so for the many students who would be tied to the pericope system later in their own practice. In addition to this, as early as the 1520s there were series of sermons on books of the Bible, especially on Matthew and John, on other days of the week. By far the majority of sermons were thus on New Testament passages, and of these the vast majority were on the Gospels.[28]

A completely different system developed in the Reformed area of the Reformation. After his arrival in Zurich in 1519 Zwingli abolished the pericope system. In long series of sermons he first dealt with Matthew, then Acts, Timothy, Galatians and Peter. This plan had a didactic aim: the community had to learn how the message of Jesus had been made known and disseminated, how Christians needed to live and what was the content of their faith. From 1525 the Old Testament came into the picture.[29] Zwingli's successor Heinrich Bullinger followed the same method. In the first twelve years of his activity in Zurich he dealt with almost all the books of the Bible.[30] The method was not only introduced throughout the Zurich area but was characteristic of Reformed Protestantism. Calvin, too, never did otherwise and implemented the system so consistently that there was no departure from it even on the great festivals. The consideration underlying this is clearly that the community has the right to hear the word of God and all the word of God. Instruction is important, and this relates to more than the main substance of Christian belief.

There are few differences in principle in the form and content of preaching throughout the Reformation movement. The preaching was clear, simple and matter-of-fact in the best sense of the word. Luther sums up his method like this. 'I avoid long introductions, and after a short prayer I read out the text without mentioning a particular theme. I then either interpret the text in order or discuss the doctrines which appear in it. Then I end with a short prayer.'[31] Calvin did the same, and avoided all rhetoric. This simplicity was the aim of all the Reformers: the content, God's own word, was so important that modesty, simplicity and restraint must be characteristics of the sermon. There are no illustrations from the lives of the saints or the Golden Legend, nor are there quotations from or allusions to classical and early Christian authors, both of which are characteristic of Catholic authors of this time. So sermons were strictly bound to the text. By contemporary standards, for all their simplicity they were academically responsible and based on an excellent philological foundation. All the Reformers used Erasmus' editions of and annotations to the New Testament and the commentaries of the early church, and some – like Bucer, Calvin and Oecolampadius, the Basle reformer – also the Jewish commentators.

It is precisely as a result of the adoption of the philological method that the present-day reader is struck by what is in another respect the pre-scientific character of the sermons. Biblical stories are seen unproblematically as accounts of what actually happened, miracles are the obvious result of God's intervention in history, the devil is as concretely active on earth as God and his angels, and the preacher need not give any reasons for treating the Gospels in a harmonizing way. Luther radically rejected as godless the still unthought-through, even unconscious beginning of the new method that we find in Erasmus: how dared Erasmus say that in Peter's speeches as recorded in the biblical book of Acts Jesus is called a man and not God, and that in the whole of the New Testament Jesus is only once called God?[32]

Here it should not be forgotten that preaching and the word of God are not only bound together in this way, but that the latter is the source from which the preaching is drawn. An identification is often made, and Luther in particular sees this in very concrete terms: the preaching of God's word is God's word. The position can also be reversed: only in preaching does the word of the Bible become the word of God.[33] That gives the preacher great weight. It can also be said that the priest becomes a preacher, without any loss of function. The preacher is as much concerned with the holy as is the priest. 'This is my body' becomes 'This is my word', and the danger of magic becomes less as a result of this shift, but is not banished.

That the sermon is the word of God did not mean that it is timeless. It often goes into specific questions, and sometimes contains fierce polemic, in which Catholicism above all suffers. Nor is that all: events in Wittenberg or Geneva were criticized, and world politics was discussed in concrete terms. Moreover there were thematic sermons; Zwingli in particular went into the questions of the day in this way. But the centre lay at a personal level: the person who is a sinner – who is justified by grace, without any merit – who moreover naturally does good works. This is the basic theme of the sermon generally, which in the Reformed tradition more than in the Lutheran was supplemented by a call to redeemed women and men to regulate their good works by the law of God. There are also further differences between the two traditions. In the Reformed tradition people had more independence as those who were socially and also politically responsible. Reformed Protestantism also had more of a city character than Lutheranism, which developed more strongly in territories governed by a local ruler. However, this remains a difference in accent.

Edifying works emerged from the practice of preaching: postillas in Lutheranism, collections of sermons in the Reformation generally. The commentaries on books of the Bible by contemporary authors and fathers of the early church were rather more remote from the centre, but sometimes also very practical by nature. In the second half of the century collections appeared, in which selected fragments of Reformation commentaries were included. But here we come right back to theology.

We have seen that the Bible was the heart of Reformation piety and the centre of worship. This also meant that it had an effect on the whole of worship. The consequences were drawn above all in the Reformed tradition. Strasbourg provides a clear example.[34] At the end of 1523 the eucharist was celebrated for the first time in two kinds and at the beginning of 1524 baptism was administered in German. After that things moved very quickly. Two years later there was only one mass per day in each of four churches. All the others were replaced by services of the word at 5, 7, 8, and 4. These contained sermons and prayers, and in some the community sang psalms translated into German. There are reports from the first months in which this last feature is mentioned as a speciality: men and women sing together from the word of God. In these same years the statues, paintings, etc., were removed from the churches; the high altar in the cathedral was replaced by a wooden table and the great crucifix was removed from the choir. In short, anything that was 'merely' external and could distract the human heart from what is essential and inward was removed. It still took about three years, up to the beginning of 1529, for the masses which remained to be replaced by a celebration of the Lord's Supper. Up to that point the two had taken place side by side, for example the celebration of the eucharist in the choir and that of the Lord's Supper in the crypt. After this change the transformation became total: no more Latin but only German; no vestments, but everyday clothes; no altar, but a table; no priest with his back to the people, but the minister turned towards the congregation; no whispered words of consecration, but a word of institution spoken in a loud voice. All this, too, accorded with the aim of the innovators: the Bible. Anything that might distract attention from that had to give way to the clear, plain word of God.

It is worth dwelling on the role of music. In Strasbourg, apart from playing the organ after the sermon as a stimulus towards reflecting on the content of the sermon, the only music was the singing of the community. There was singing of psalms translated into German rhyming verse, supplemented with a number of hymns, above all at festivals. This rule was less rigorous than for example in Zurich, where all music was banned.[35] Nevertheless, here, too, there was an almost manic concentration on the Bible. Even the response of human beings to the salvation of God had by preference to be drawn directly from the Bible. Through Calvin, who served refugees in Strasbourg between 1538 and 1541 as a preacher for the French Reformed refugees, this practice came to predominate in the Reformed family of churches, so that for centuries it was as characteristic and formative of the community as was the Latin mass for Catholicism.

What value did the Bible have for the innovators of the sixteenth century? In 1524 the printer of a Dutch translation of the New Testament put it in an incomparable way when he said that God 'has at last had mercy on the hungry crowd, has put an end to sorrow and fed them with the heavenly living bread of his divine word'.[36]

Translated by John Bowden

Notes

1. *Opus epistolarum Desiderii Erasmi Roterodami*, ed. P. S. Allen, 2, Oxford 1910, Ep. 384, 42–9.

2. For this see generally C. Augustijn, *Erasmus*, Baarn 1986; G. Bedouelle and B. Roussel, *Le temps des Réformes et La Bible*, Bible de tous les temps 51, Paris 1989.

3. See L. Geiger, *Johann Reuchlins Briefwechsel*, Stuttgart 1875 = Hildesheim 1962, Ep. 115, 123.

4. See Bernd Moeller, 'Frömmigkeit in Deutschland um 1500', in *Archiv für Reformationsgeschichte* 56, 1965, 5–31.

5. Heidelberg Catechism, question and answer 98, in J. N. Bakhuizen van den Brink, *Den Nederlandse belijdenisgeschriften in authentieke teksten*, second edition, Amsterdam 1976, 206–7.

6. F. Lau and E. Bizer, *Reformationsgeschichte Deutschlands bis 1555*, Kirche in ihrer Geschichte 3, Göttingen 1964, K 59.

7. See C. Augustijn, 'Allein das heilig evangelium. Het mandaat van het Reichsregiment 6 maart 1523', in *Nederlands Archief voor Kerkgeschiedenis*, NS 48, 1968, 150–65.

8. See the summary in *Theologische Realenzyklopädie* 6, Berlin and New York 1980, 228–66.

9. One example is provided by the Louvain heresy trials of 1543. See C.–A. Campan, *Mémoires de Frrancisco de Enzinas . . . 1543–1545*, Vol.I.2 (*Pieces justificatives*), Brussels and La Haye 1862. All those involved had a Bible and this was expounded in small house-meetings or in the open air.

10. The expression is that of the South-Netherlands Reformed preacher Petrus Datheen; see A. J. Jelsma, *Adriaan van Haemstede en zijn martelaarsboek*, The Hague 1970, 35.

11. For the Netherlands see e.g. C. A. van Swigchem, T. Brouwer and W. van Os, *Een huis voor het Woord. Het protestantse kerkinterieur in Nederland tot 1900*, The Hague 1984.

13. See L. F. Groenendijk, *De Nadere Reformatie van het gezin. De visie van Petrus Wittewrongel op de christelijke huishouding*, Dordrecht nd [1984], 47f.

13. See M. Brecht, *Martin Luther. Sein Weg zur Reformation 1483–1521*, Second edition, Stuttgart 1983, 162, 266–70.

14. For him see S. Wiedenhofer, *Formalstrukturen humanistischer und reformatorischer Theologie bei Philipp Melanchthon*, Regensburger Studien zur Theologie 2, two vols., Berne, Frankfurt am Main and Munich 1976.

15. See H. J. de Jonge, 'Erasmus und die Glossa Ordinaria zum Neuen Testament', in *Nederlands Archief voor Kerkgeschiedenis*, NS 56, 1975, 51–77.

16. See Melanchthon's *Werke in Auswahl*, ed. R. Stupperich, Vol. 5, Gütersloh 1965, esp. 373–8.

17. Martin Luther, *Werke. Kritische Gesamtausgabe* (WA), Vols. 42–44, Weimar 1911, 1912, 1915.

18. In his 'Sendbrief vom Dolmetschen' (1530), see WA 30, II, 1909, 627–46.

19. Luther, WA 42, 1911, 190.30–192.13.

20. Calvin, for example, began his activity as a biblical exegete in Geneva in the autumn of 1536 by expounding the Letter to the Romans. His first commentary on a book of the Bible was also devoted to this work (1540). See Jean Calvin, *Commentarius in Epistolam ad Romanos*, ed. T. H. L. Parker, Studies in the History of Christian Thought 22, Leiden 1981, IX–X.

21. M. Bucer, *S. Psalmorum libri quinque ad ebraicam veritatem versi et familiari explanatione elucidati*, Argentorati 1529.

22. See J. V. Pollet, *Martin Bucer. Etudes sur les relations de Bucer avec les Pays-bas*, Vol.2, Studies in Medieval and Reformation Thought 34, Leiden 1985, no.2, 19–212.

23. Jean Calvin, *Opera quae supersunt omnia*, Vol.10, II, Corpus Reformatorum 38 II, Brunswick 1872, no.87, ch.143.

24. See I. Gäbler, *Huldrych Zwingli. Eine Einführung in sein Leben und sein Werk*, Beck'sche Elementarbücher, Munich 1983, 92f.

25. See A. A. van Schelven, *De Nederduitsche vluchtelingenkerken der XVIe eeuw in Engeland en Duitschland in hunne beteekenis voor de reformatie in de Nederlanden*, The Hague 1909, 85–9.

26. See P. Fraenkel, *De l'écriture à la dispute. Le cas de l'Académie de Genève sous Théodore de Bèze*, Cahiers de la Revue de Theologie et de Philosophie 1, Lausanne 1977.

27. See G. Bedouelle, *Lefevre d'Étaples et l'Intelligence des écritures*, Travaux d'Humanisme et Rénaissance 152, Geneva 1976.

28. See G. Ebeling, *Evangelische Evangelienauslegung. Eine Untersuchung zu*

Luthers Hermeneutik, Forschungen zur Geschichte und Lehre des Protestantismus X.1, Munich 1942 = Darmstadt 1962, 21–5.

29. See O. Farner, *Huldrych Zwingli*, Vol.3, Zurich 1954, 36–45.

30. For him see W. Hollweg, *Heinrich Bullingers Hausbuch. Eine Untersuchung über die Anfänge der reformierten Predigtliteratur*, Beiträge zur Geschichte und Lehre der Reformierten Kirche 8, Neukirchen 1956.

31. See Ebeling, *Evangelienauslegung* (n.28), 26.

32. Luther, WA 7 (*Briefwechsel*), no.2093, 122–4, 206–23.

33. See E. Winkler, 'Luther als Seelsorger und Prediger', in H. Junghans (ed.), *Leben und Werk Martin Luthers von 1526–1545*, 1, Göttingen 1983, 235f. See also already *De servo arbitrio*, in Luther, WA 18, 1908, 653. 22–35.

34. For what follows see R. Bornert, *Le réforme protestante du culte à Strasbourg au XVIe siècle (1523–1598). Approche sociologique et interprétation théologique*, Studies in Mediaeval and Reformation Thought 27, Leiden 1981.

35. See Gäbler, *Zwingli*, 97.

36. Quoted in S. W. Bijl, *Erasmus in het Nederlands tot 1617* (no place or date [1978]), 34.

Biblical Studies in the Eighteenth Century. From the Letter to the Figure

Jean-Robert Armogathe

Recent research[1] has led to a revision of received ideas about biblical studies in the eighteenth century: hitherto they were regarded only as textual criticism, seen as a novelty and a progress. However, criticism and interpretation clash and cross: does scholarly examination of the texts allow the imposition of a unique literal sense, or is it proper to resort to spiritual and symbolic, figurative readings of scripture? The debate is an old one, but the century of the Enlightenment allows us to put it sharply, beginning from a wider experience of textual criticism. The work of Richard Simon would then appear as the product of a critical effort pursued by the Catholics since the Tridentine decree of April 1546: to wreck the verbal inspiration of the scriptures by the accumulation of textual problems. The Prolegomena that Brian Walton, Bishop of Chester, suggests at the beginning of his Polyglot Bible (London 1657) contain the essentials of the modern contribution. Taking them up in 1707, John Mill was able to suggest thirty thousand textual variants in the New Testament. He is the first editor of the Greek text to have described its manuscripts precisely and clearly; not content with just giving variants, he judged their value, and he is the first to have attempted a genealogy of editions (he recognized his debt to Richard Simon in the case of the ancient versions). However, in spite of this learned work, Mill did not believe that he could modify the received text, and he reproduced the third edition by Estienne, contenting himself with indicating and classifying the variants and notes (and often he prefers the variant closest to the Vulgate).

We owe the basic modern Greek text of the New Testament to Johannes Albert Bengel (1667–1752): one could date the birth of modern exegesis to

1734, the year in which it was published. However, his work benefited from many earlier contributions, French and English. Bengel had become an exegete, as he recalls, *per tentationem*, because he was tempted in his faith by the variants in the texts of the Gospels. His work is methodical and made it possible to dissipate in Protestant circles the atmosphere of suspicion surrounding biblical criticism. An irreproachable churchman and a Württemberg pietist, Bengel sometimes chose his versions by inner inspiration; his principle was: 'add nothing to scripture but leave none of it obscure'. Scripture for him was not 'a dumb oracle': in the religious tradition of German pietism he read in it the 'incomparable story of the divine government of humanity down the ages of the world, from the beginning to the end of all things'. His *Gnomon Novi Testamenti* (1742) is a model of science, but it is also a spiritual writing, as was recognized by John Wesley (*Notes on the New Testament*, 1755). In it Bengel comments at length on the Pastoral Epistles and attaches special importance to the Apocalypse. Bengal's criticism is the direct outcome of pietistic interpretation: to reach the tasty kernel of the scriptures it is proper that critical science should first break the shell (a distinction made by A. H. Francke in his *Manuductio*, 1693). To arrive at this kernel it is necessary to know the ancient languages: the eighteenth century saw a spread in the chairs of Hebrew, in linguistic methods and working tools. But it is not just a matter of understanding the words; it is also necessary to understand the significance of phrases. Francke introduces an essential distinction between *sensus literalis* and *sensus literae*: the literal sense is what the words engender in their own original sense; it is not concerned with exegetical reading but strictly relates only to philological reading, 'that which concerns the shell' (and not the kernel, the literal sense of which is exclusively the concern of exegetical reading).

'Thou shalt not kill': the meaning intended by the Holy Spirit is not limited to the grammatical reality (a prohibition of murder), but also extends to violence, wounds and mutilations.

Grammar is not enough for understanding the meaning of the scriptures: it is also necessary to know rhetoric and to resort to the *affectus*. The *lectio simplex* comes into its own once the underlying text, released by scientific apparatus, appears to reveal itself to the believer.

The pietistic current constantly finds itself caught between rationalist criticisms, whose scientific concern it shares, and enlightened readings, the inspired status of which it accepts. Jews, Catholics, Protestants and Orthodox: all the people of the Book are traversed by identical currents, rending scholarly opinion between mystical, kabbalistic and allegorical interpretations and the work of textual criticism.

The churches encouraged, held back, tried to control the movement:

the authorities in Berlin and the Walloon ministers in Holland banned the *New Testament* of Jean Le Clerc (1703), who wanted to keep clear of all dogmatic reading. However, Le Clerc challenged Richard Simon with his principles of interpretation:

> To tell the history of a book is not simply to say when and by whom it was made, what copyists transmitted it and what mistakes they made in transcribing it. It is not enough to tell us who translated it and to draw our attention to the faults in his version, nor even to teach us who commented on it and the defects in these commentaries. We also have to discover, if that is possible, to what end the author composed it, what occasion made him take up his pen and to what opinions or events he may be referring in this work, above all when this is not a book which contains general reflections or eternal truths which are the same in all ccenturies and among all the people of the world (*Sentiments de quelques théologiens de Hollande*, first letter, 1686).

In 1711 a pastor, Hennig Bernhard Witter, discovered different traditions in the Pentateuch. His hypothesis was taken up and developed by a Catholic, Jean Astruc, whose *Conjectures on the Original Memorials of which Moses seems to have made use in composing the Book of Genesis* (1753) was put on the index. He had to move to Germany, but there Richard Simon encountered strong resistance and it was not until 1776 that a German translation of his *Critical History of the New Testament* (1676) appeared. Astruc was translated in his turn, in 1783, and his hypothesis, developed from the diversity of styles (that Witter had already noted) reactivated the study of the Pentateuch in the person of J. G. Eichhorn (1752–1849).

In talking of developments in rationalist criticism it is necessary to distinguish between periods: Reimarus, Paulus (1761–1851) and Strauss (1808–74) all deny the miracles, but the two former stress the factual account and look for explanations: if for Reimarus the miracles are tricks, Paulus looks for their natural causes. Strauss doubted the historical reality itself, and his 'mythical' explanation, by virtue of its psychological and sociological consideration, goes beyond the realism of the two others.

In the name of pure reason, against a theory of divine revelation, Hermann Samuel Reimarus had written his *Apologia* (*Apologie, oder Schutzschrift für die vernünftigen Verehrer Gottes*), partly published between 1774 and 1777 by Lessing (Fragments of a Wolfenbüttel Anonymous).

Paulus's life of Jesus, which appeared in 1828, is a good example of a 'positivist' explanation of the Gospel miracles: without denying the historicity of the facts reported, Paulus stripped them of all supernatural character. The blind were healed by an eye-lotion, the demon-possessed by diet and by the 'psychic force' of Jesus; the dead were 'raised' from an apparent death, but not a clinical death. The sum total of pedantic details given by Paulus ends up, despite his protestations, in making Jesus a kind of charlatan. Moreover rationalist criticism was very hard on Paulus, in whose work 'the moral dignity of Jesus is difficult to defend' (K. A. von Hase, 1891), while Renan judged his explanations 'ridiculous and puerile'. However, they made their mark, and even if the name of Paulus is forgotten today, 'his ideas still travel in all kinds of disguises in the commentaries on the life of Jesus', as Albert Schweitzer put it.

J. S. Semler (1752–1791) departed from traditional biblical theology, and Baur borrowed from him the idea of a distinction between Jewish Christianity and Gentile Christianity. Semler was not content to challenge the disputed passages of scripture (the contradictions between the Gospels, for example), but put in doubt the historicity of numerous passages, including the sayings of Jesus in the Gospels which coincide. However, Semler never wanted to break with orthodoxy, and he supported Wöllner's edict.

It was in order to react to Semler's rationalist attempt that Herder decided to adapt into German (1783) the study by the Anglican bishop Robert Lowth (1710–1787) *On the Sacred Poetry of the Hebrews* (*De sacra poesi hebraeorum*, 1753). Lowth had given eloquent lectures, in Latin, in which he extolled the riches of biblical poetry, the delicacy of its sentiments and the originality of its form. The enthusiastic adaptation by Herder had a considerable influence on Romantic German poetry.

Furthermore, the influence of Spinoza and his circle must not be underestimated. Christ is mentioned about a hundred times in the *Tractatus Theologico-politicus* (1670): Spinoza had a clear intellectual vision of God and knew by understanding what the prophets knew by imagination. However, Spinoza's christology, through contact with Dutch Christian dissidents, rejected the incarnation: the wisdom of God is manifested by the *mens*, the spirit of Christ, which is God in a man. In his letters to Oldenburg, Spinoza develops his idea and draws the consequences: history teaches us that Jesus lived and died, but the stories of the resurrection have to be taken in a spiritual sense. Rationalist criticism went further, above all among the English Deists: reacting against the literalism of Abraham Calov (*Biblia Illustrata*, 1672) and of Dom Calmet (1720), criticism first attacked the miracles (Hume, Woolston) and then the history of scripture (Collins, Voltaire, d'Holbach).

The debate on prophecy is particularly interesting: Anthony Collins tried to show that the Old Testament prophecies were false and had never been realized. To that end he put forward a thesis on the historicity of the prophecies, formulated in the following way: 'All the ancient prophecies expressly referred to Jesus Christ.' Thomas Sherlock replied to him in his book on the prophets (1725): he suggested another formulation (which in fact is very modern): 'All that God announced to our fathers in terms of salvation is perfectly accomplished in Jesus Christ.' The same Sherlock published against Woolston an essay on the resurrection of Jesus (*The Trial of the Witnesses to the Resurrection*, 1729) which defended the historicity of scripture but without supporting the literal meaning.

Thus the two permanent poles of any reading of the scriptures came face to face: critical effort, seeking to arrive at the substance of the text, and symbolic effort, seeking to decipher the figurative, metaphorical or spiritual meanings behind the letter.

J. D. Michaelis's *Introduction to the Divine Writings of the New Covenant* dominates this eighteenth century (the fourth edition was published in 1788), and its influence extended into the next century: Herbert Marsh translated it into English in 1793 with important additions; the edition edited by Rosenmüller in 1795 contains the German translation of Marsh's remarks, which were taken up in the French translation of Pastor Chenevière (1822). Michaelis set out to reply to the objections derived from the 'contradictions' in scripture: his critical and philological survey takes account of Bengal's achievements. Above all, Michaelis counters the attempts at reductions and dismemberment with a coherent vision of revelation in scripture. He was highly successful with the Catholics: J. L. Hug of Freiburg, whose own *Introduction to the Writings of the New Testament* went through four editions between 1808 and 1847, or Abbé Garnier, who trained several generations of priests (including Ernest Renan) at St Sulpice between 1803 and 1845; his scientific posterity was assured by his pupil Abbé Glaire, who taught Holy Scripture at the Sorbonne from 1825.

The 'tradition of the fathers' made it possible to resort to other readings: the patristic renewal of the seventeenth century explains how Dom Martianay could propose in 1704 a *Methodical Treatise or Way of Explaining Scripture with the Help of Three Syntaxes: Proper, Figured and Harmonic*. Of the different spiritual senses, the main one is what Martianay calls *allegorical*;[2] the central idea is that the Old Testament is as it were the *figure* of the New: the promises made to Israel are the images of eternal benefits brought by Christ to his church. Abbé Bergier (1718–1790) set out to collect articles for a *Theological Dictionary* to complete (and revise) the theological content of the *Encyclopédie* (in the *Encyclopédie méthodique* of 1788); he defended himself against having plagiarized the *Dictionary of the Bible* by Dom Calmet (1672–1757), and in fact his method is quite different. More than a generation separates the

Benedictine from Lorraine and the apologist from France Comté. Calmet gives a literal commentary on scripture. A good example is his article 'Parable', which is quite short: he retains above all the probable historicity of certain parables (the good Samaritan, the prodigal son, Lazarus and the rich man, the king who leaves for a distant country); by contrast, Bergier stresses the fact that 'when it comes to parables, one must not press all the terms nor require that the allegory should be always sustained'. In Mark 11;13, the episode of the fig tree cursed by Jesus because it bore no fruit 'when it was not the season for figs' has always exercised the perspicacity of exegetes. Calmet tries to find in Pliny and Theophrastus a kind of early fig which comes before the usual season for figs, an ingenious and erudite solution which Bergier mentions but does not dwell on. The struggle over *figurism* dominated the whole century, and that explains why the Dominican authors of the *Universal Dictionary of the Ecclesiastical Sciences* (1759–1765) defend a narrow literalism in commentary and the *verbal* inspiration of the Scriptures: 'Holy Scripture has been inspired not only in things but also in all that it says.'

In this way they are opposed both to the Jesuits (who follow Bellarmine's theory of the simple *aid* of the Holy Spirit) and the 'figurists', the principal theoretician among whom is the Jansenist Abbé Duguet, to whom has been attributed the anonymous *Rules for Understanding the Scriptures* (1716). The history of this work and its vast posterity, with the abbot of Etemare and in convulsionary and millenarian circles, is a complex one. What needs to be remembered is that the quest to renew patristic exegesis resulted in its total transformation. In fact for the fathers the events of the past were 'figures', for all that they were 'allegorical': the temporal benefits which accrued to Israel are figures of the spiritual benefits which must accrue to the new Israel. Figurism abolishes the 'vertical' aspect; temporal hope will be realized in a historical, political and social future. This purely temporal, linear exegesis has had a long posterity, and comes from the figurist debates of the eighteenth century.

In conclusion, the 'Isenbiehl affair' allows us to see what was really at stake. Johannes Lorenz Isenbiehl (1744–1818) was a Catholic priest who was taught at Göttingen by J. D. Michaelis. In his German thesis of 1774, published in 1778 (*A New Attempt on the Emmanuel Prophecy*), Isenbiehl argued that the passage on 'the virgin (*almah*) who shall conceive' (Isa. 7.14) cannot be understood to be the Virgin Mary (far less could it serve to prove the virginity of Mary). Translated into Latin, the work was condemned by the Sorbonne (1778) and then, a year later, by a letter of Pius VI (*Divina Christi Domini Voce*). The Roman text condemned the work because its author rejected the *literal sense* and the mystical sense of the prophetic text. Orthodox exegesis was in fact careful to preserve the

literal sense. Jean Martianay remained scornful of the 'falsely Enlightened', 'many theologians and a large number of preachers who
imagine that they see everywhere in scripture only senses that they call
mystical'. The lasting success of Dom Calmet is in this obsessive concern
for the literal sense, 'the foundation for all the other explanations' (1720).
The role of the prophetic texts in the discussions with the Socinians and
the Jews is essential for understanding this concern. The double significance of the prophecies retained by Grotius is perceived as being dangerous for dogma, and damaging to apologetic.

The Jesuit Jean-Francois Baltus (1667–1743) devotes two volumes to
defending the prophets against Grotius:

> Grotius is certainly wrong and one knows only too well why he thus
> turns the clearest prophecies and the literal shapes into allegories, but
> those who follow him among the Catholics, who are so prejudiced in his
> favour, are incomparably more wrong than he, since in adopting his
> ideas they visibly favour the impiety of the Socinians (in *Mémoires de
> Trevoux*, March 1738, 524).

Only the literal sense can be the basis of dogma, prove it and explain it,
and what more can one ask of scripture? This exegesis would seem
curiously to fall short of the decisions of the Council of Trent and the
scriptural theories of Bellarmine: among the Catholics one has to listen to
Newman to rediscover the intuitions of the sixteenth century. In fact
Baltus attacked Richard Simon for having claimed to substitute the
miracles for the prophecies in their function as proof, a criticism which
equally applies to the *Pensées* of Pascal. To favour the miracles by
reducing the prophecies to historical reminiscences made in the past
tended to favour the opponents of the constitution *Unigenitus*; the
healings performed on the tomb of the deacon Paris tended to prove his
cause. By devaluing the prophecies, and undermining the literal sense, in a
way Richard Simon had prepared the way for the figurist exegetes.

Eighteenth-century biblical criticism is full of contrasts: the critical
movement started by Erasmus expanded and filled out. New instruments
were set in place, and above all rules of method, starting from the criticism
of secular texts and taking account of the specific nature of the biblical
corpus. The knowledge of Hebrew and Samaritan, a more archaeological
approach to the Holy Land (which was to lead to the creation of the
Palestine Association in London in 1804), makes it possible to discern the
literal sense of the text more easily. In fact 'biblical science', the great
Commentaries of Dom Calmet (rather than his Dictionary, which was
more summary), adds up to something which can still be used today. The

theories about the formation and history of texts fall into place, and the idea of tradition is consequently made deeper.

However, alongside these scientific and critical developments, interpretation came to have a comparable importance. It fed on the patristic traditions, but also on the renewal of rhetoric. Figurism is excessive, but takes account of a horizon of thought in which the Bible is a factor in imagination and calculation.

Those are the two faces of the eighteenth century: the side of the 'Enlightenment' and the 'shadow' side (though that is often 'enlightened'). Its richness and diversity are the best pledges of later developments, which were also greatly contrasting, in biblical study.

Translated by John Bowden

Notes

1. This study owes much to two thick volumes of *La Bible de Tous les Temps*: Vol.6, *Le Grand Siècle et la Bible*, edited by J.-R. Armogathe (Paris 1989, 836pp.), and Vol.7, *Le Siècle des Lumières et la Bible*, edited by Yvon Belaval and Dominique Bourel (Paris 1986, 870pp.).

2. In this connection Hervé Simon recalls that this 'allegorical' sense is what is nowadays called 'typology', while 'allegory' would consist more of looking in scripture for symbols of psychological, moral and cosmological realities (*Le Grand Siècle et la Bible*, 758).

III · The Bible the Soul of the Contemporary Church?

The Magisterium and the Bible: North American Experience

Christine E. Gudorf

One of the most striking changes in the Roman Catholic church in North America since Vatican II is enthusiastic lay response to the urging of individual Bible reading. The laity are, however, confronted with two very different approaches to the Bible, one very traditional, largely literalist approach given to proof-texting and neglect of biblical scholarship, and one based on the Catholic biblical scholarship unleashed by Pius XII's *Divino afflante Spiritu* of 1943.[1] This unleashing of Catholic biblical scholars has been technically honoured in so far as there have been no biblical scholars among those theologians whose orthodoxy has been investigated, but hopes that this new freedom would lead the *magisterium* to address, evaluate and appropriate fruits of biblical scholarship have gone largely unfulfilled.

The majority of Catholic laity in North America still view Jesus in docetic terms, as uninfluenced by and rejecting of Judaism, as having preached an otherworldly and individualistic heaven and the unimportance of materiality. They interpret the claim that the Bible is one of two sources of revelation to mean that it is internally consistent, historically accurate, and an infallible guide for moral behaviour, whose truths are self-evident. The *magisterium* rarely addresses such misinterpretations or teaches scripture directly, thus leaving popular misunderstandings unchallenged.

I will here examine three major expressions of magisterial Bible use relevant to North America: 1. papal teaching: 2. documents of the Congregation for the Doctrine of the Faith (CDF), and 3. pastoral teaching of the North American bishops.

John Paul II's use of the Bible

Treatment of papal *magisterium* is here confined to that of John Paul II. An examination of his teaching reveals a consistent message that: 1. all need catechesis based on the word of God located in scripture and tradition,[2] and 2. while it is biblical scholarship which makes the distinction between what is obsolete and what is always valuable in scripture,[3] biblical scholars function in service to the *magisterium*[4] which decides what biblical scholarship is merely the opinions of biblical scholars and what is authoritative.[5] Yet John Paul II never directly addresses the Bible or biblical scholarship, leaving unclear what is authoritative and what is opinion.

In the wake of the pastoral upheaval following the implementation of Vatican II's extensive reforms John Paul II tends to avoid that which could confuse, undermine faith in the church, or scandalize the simplest of the laity. This tendency determines what aspects of biblical scholarship are adopted by the papal *magisterium*. Thus John Paul II proposed the celebration of 1983 as the 1950th anniversary of the redemption of humanity without any reference to the general consensus of scholars that Jesus was not born in the year 1, and did not die in 33, but rather earlier.[6] Of course, the date has no ability to alter the meaning of the redemption. Yet the failure to correct this common historical misconception serves to maintain lay attitudes about the absolute facticity of both scripture and tradition – attitudes which create obstacles for the development of strong, mature faith.

John Paul II is not loath to display some knowledge of recent scripture scholarship; as Karl Rahner noted, John Paul II 'spoke publicly of the Yahwist, and seventy years ago we didn't deal very kindly with the exegete who used the same expression!'[7] John Paul II approved the 'Notes on the Jews and Jesus in Preaching and Catechesis' of the Vatican Commission for Relations with the Jews, which integrates much biblical scholarship into its presentation of the Jewish roots of Christianity and the New Testament treatment of Jews.[8] In his own addresses to those involved in Jewish-Christian dialogue there is a detectable weakening of the stance found in the 'Notes', though he repeats his approval of that document.[9] But even this somewhat weakened stance on the Jewish roots of Jesus and the intrinsic relation of Christianity and Judaism is absent from his teaching aimed at the Catholic laity, who are not led to question what they view as the radical originality of Christ's teaching.

John Paul II is not so prone as many of his predecessors to stud his addresses with brief unnecessary phrases quoted without explanation from scripture, though he does on occasion:

> drawing with wisdom from the treasury of the church 'things old and new' (Matt. 13.52).[10]

> collaborating with the bishop, in a spirit of unity and 'obedience of faith' (Rom. 1.5).[11]

Occasionally the context of such brief quotations is less apt, as when we wrote:

> No Christian, especially those with titles signifying a special conse-
> cration in the church, should become responsible for breaking this
> unity, acting outside or against the will of the bishops, 'whom the Holy
> Spirit has set to guide the Church of God' (Acts 20.28).[12]

The reference in Acts is to 'elders' of the church in Ephesus, not 'bishops', whose office was unknown in Acts.

John Paul II also uses entire biblical stories to structure his documents, such as that of the rich young man in his 1985 letter to world youth,[13] or that of the Good Samaritan in 'To Listen to Our Neighbour'.[14] The Genesis creation story similarly forms the basis for the normative approach to work in *Laborem exercens*,[15] followed by an examination of Jesus' positive attitude towards work through his trade, his ministry, and his many references to work in parables. *Dives in Misericordia* offers an extensive survey of scripture on its theme of mercy, though it draws on tradition rather than biblical scholarship for interpretation.[16]

In his homily closing the 1987 Synod, John Paul II ignored biblical scholarship when he interpreted Mark 3.32–35 as if Jesus here *honoured* his mother and brothers instead of denying them.[17] Also ignored are Jesus' repeated repudiations of the priority of the natural family.[18] In *Redemptoris Mater* John Paul II treats this same incident along with Jesus' reply to the woman in Luke 11:27–28 who cried out, 'Blessed is the womb that bore you, and the breasts that gave you suck!':

> Is Jesus thereby distancing himself from his mother according to the
> flesh? Does he perhaps wish to leave her in the hidden obscurity which
> she herself has chosen? If this seems to be the case from the tone of these
> words, one must nevertheless note that the new and different mother-
> hood which Jesus speaks of to his disciples refers precisely to Mary in a
> very special way. Is not Mary the first of 'those who hear the word of
> God and do it?' . . . Thus we can say that the blessing proclaimed by
> Jesus is not in opposition, despite appearances, to the blessing uttered
> by the unknown woman, but rather coincides with that blessing in the
> person of the Virgin mother, who called herself only 'the handmaid of
> the Lord' (Luke 1.38).[19]

In both documents John Paul II assumes without biblical basis the discipleship of Mary during Jesus' ministry, insisting that Jesus' re-pudiation of the primacy of kin did not include her. He ignores completely an earlier verse in Mark 3: 'And when his family heard it, they went out to seize him, for people were saying "He is beside himself"' (3:21) and the possibility that such seizure, however well intentioned, was contrary to Jesus' will.

Bible use by the Congregation for the Doctrine of the Faith

The Congregation for the Doctrine of the Faith (CDF) functions to protect the *magisterium* by correcting and disciplining those who question or deny it. The CDF acts for the pope, who approves its decrees. Its function is essentially a conservative one; when a pope teaches a new concept, the CDF, in collaboration with the pope, decides what are acceptable and unacceptable interpretations and extensions of such teaching, in the light of previous magisterial teaching. The CDF is, not surprisingly, less inclined to use contemporary scripture scholarship, tending to defend traditional theology with traditional biblical props. I will refer to CDF documents after 1975, including some from the pontificate of Paul VI.

The CDF is much more inclined than John Paul II to traditional studding of its arguments with brief biblical quotations not necessary to its argument, as in: 'Faith in the Incarnate Word dead and risen for all men and whom "God made Lord and Christ" (Acts 2.36) is denied.'[20] The CDF here charges that the claim of liberation theology that one can meet the 'Jesus of history in the revolutionary struggle of the poor for liberation' denies faith in the Incarnate Word. The Acts 2 quotation adds nothing to the argument, for no one denied that God made Jesus Lord and Christ. There is a similar use in the 'Declaration on the Question of the Admission of Women to the Ministerial Priesthood'. 'When "the fullness of time comes" (Gal. 4.4), the Word, the Son of God, takes on flesh . . .'[21] Studding arguments with biblical quotations irrelevant to the argument functions to give the appearance of biblical support for the overall argument.

CDF documents also use biblical passages to support principal points of their argument: 'God's love, poured out into our hearts by the Holy Spirit, involves love of neighbour. Recalling the First Commandment, Jesus immediately adds: "and the second is like it, You shall love your neighbour as yourself" (Matt. 22.29–30)'.[22] The quotation is apt, but when such uses constitute the principal method of teaching the laity the Bible, they can misrepresent the Bible's message about Jesus. Jesus' first commandment was taken in entirety from the Shema, the most important Jewish prayer; the second was known to the Essenes from the *Testament of the Twelve Patriarchs*, and supported by Rabbi Hillel in rabbinic circles.[23] This accounts for the scribe's quick approval in Mark 12.32–33. Use of the quotation here, without further explanation, allows the laity to persist in understanding this teaching as original to Jesus, an exclusively Christian teaching.

A much clearer misuse is: 'They [the Beatitudes] also divert us from an unrealistic and ruinous search for a perfect world, "for the form of this world is passing away" (1 Cor. 7.31).'[24] This quotation comes from a time when the early church expected an imminent second coming;[25] earlier Paul urges no changes in marital status, since the short time remaining should be spent in preparation. This imminent expectation disappeared during the second century; thus the church continues to marry and annul. More importantly, use of this quotation supports the popular misunderstanding of Jesus' kingdom as a totally otherworldly, spiritualistic one. Such thinking ignores the Jewish roots of Jesus' proclamation, as well as the teaching of the early church, continued in the creeds and in Vatican II,[26] that the second coming would initiate a general bodily resurrection of all the dead, judgment, and a new earth for those passing judgment.

Another example:

> Thus, instead of seeing, with St Paul, a figure of baptism in the Exodus (I Cor. 10.1–2), some end up making of it a symbol of the political liberation of a people.[27]

I Cor. 10.1–2 reads: 'I want you to know, brethren, that our fathers were all under the cloud, and all passed through the sea, and all were baptized into Moses in the cloud and in the sea . . .' Paul was not rejecting the political implications of the Exodus. Christian adoption of the Old Testament from Hebrew scriptures included adoption of Jewish interpretations of the Exodus as uniting political and spiritual liberation. Forcing a choice between one insignificant, undeveloped biblical quotation which finds a baptismal symbol in Exodus and the meaning of the overall story of Exodus for millennia of Jewish and Christian history is absurd. The Exodus was the beginning of the nation Israel; the very title of Messiah and the roots of the kingdom Jesus died announcing are inseparable historically from the political interpretation of Exodus.

Sometimes the CDF makes problematic references to specific Bible passages without quotations, as in the 'Declaration on Certain Questions Concerning Sexual Ethics': 'In sacred Scripture they [homosexual acts] are condemned as serious depravity and even presented as the sad consequence of rejecting God (Rom. 1.24–27; I Cor. 6.10; I Tim. 1.10).'[28] The problem here is literalism. The Declaration recognized the social scientific consensus that true homosexuality, as opposed to that rooted in false education, habit or bad example, is not primarily a behaviour, but an innate orientation, which, once set, is irreversible.[29] Paul condemned homosexual *acts* which he understood as rebellion against a natural, God-given heterosexual orientation. Allowing Paul's ignorance to define moral and immoral behaviour is analogous to demanding belief in an imminent second coming because Paul and the New Testament so believed.

The CDF further elaborated its approach to scripture with reference to homosexuality in its 1986 'Letter to the Bishops of the Catholic Church on the Pastoral Care of Homosexual Persons':

> It is likewise essential to recognize that the Scriptures are not properly understood when they are interpreted in a way which contradicts the Church's living Tradition. To be correct, the interpretation of scripture must be in substantial accord with that Tradition.[30]

This approach prevents interpretation of the Bible from initiating new developments in church tradition. It is also in tension with John Paul II's teaching that biblical scholars differentiate the obsolete from the always valuable in the Bible, for here the CDF rejects an interpretation of biblical scholars not on the basis of their scholarly assessment of obsolete and valuable, but on the basis of whether their interpretation agrees with tradition.

The Profession of Faith, which, with the Oath of Fidelity, was designed and promulgated by the CDF in 1989, implicitly demands that teachers of Catholic morality and theology in seminaries and Catholic universities ignore the history of development within both Bible and tradition:

> With firm faith I believe as well everything contained in the word of God, written or handed down in tradition and proposed by the church . . . as divinely revealed and calling for faith.[31]

The CDF's latest offering, *Catechism for the Universal Church*, circulating among the bishops for comments in early 1990, has drawn early and especially strong criticism for its inadequate use of the Bible.[32]

The CDF clearly betrays no hesitation in utilizing scripture while rejecting completely biblical scholarship and insisting on both the authority of all parts of the Bible and the impossibility of contradiction between Bible and tradition.

The North American bishops

The bishops' conferences in North America seem slightly more inclined to teach the Bible than the pope or the CDF. The most direct approach to the Bible is found in the Canadian Conference of Catholic Bishops' (CCCB) 'Jesus Christ: The Centre of Christian Life', which surveys Jesus' ministry, death and resurrection in the Bible.[33] A major section is devoted to biblical evidence for the fullness of Jesus' humanity, and includes a treatment of Jesus' knowledge and human self-consciousness, and a recognition of the different levels of developing christology in the New Testament. Although inspired by John Paul II's *Redemptor Hominis*,[34] which also attempts to integrate biblical evidence with tradition, the bishops use New Testament scholarship as the framework for the integration, while John Paul II largely ignores biblical scholarship in favour of occasional short biblical quotations. The bishops refute popular but heretical docetic interpretations of Jesus Christ, and stress the kingdom of God as key to the New Testament witness. In this document the bishops here exemplify the approach advocated in their 'A Reflection on Moral Living', which urges heavy reliance on the word of God, especially the Gospels, among laity. The words of the Sermon on the Mount, they say:

> . . . do not tell us what to do in every situation, but they point the way. . . . Only if we reflect deeply and prayerfully on the challenge of the Gospel will we transform our hearts and follow the right path.
>
> The Bible is not the only guide for our conscience in the complex and ever changing circumstances of our lives. God's word lives on throughout the ages in the community of those who believe in Jesus Christ . . .[35]

The bishops thus urge the Bible as a primary guide, augmented by church tradition, but oppose both literalism and legalistic approaches to the Bible so prevalent among the laity.

Over the past two decades the documents of both US and Canadian bishops' conferences have developed a new style: documents have become longer documents, more inclusive of social analysis, less juridical and more pastoral. Some documents survey biblical attitudes relevant to a particular topic, attempting to demonstrate a dominant biblical perspective on the topic. This is typical of the US Catholic Conference's (USCC) 'The Challenge of Peace'[36] and 'Economic Justice for All',[37] the Canadian bishops' (CCCB) 'New Hope in Christ: A Pastoral Message on Sickness and Healing',[38] and, to a lesser extent, their 'Ethical Reflections on the Economic Crisis'.[39]

'The Challenge of Peace' prefaces its biblical survey by stating: 1. the appropriateness of believers looking to scripture for guidance; 2. the complexity posed by the many meanings of peace in scripture; 3. that the Bible reflects varied historical situations and times all different from our own; and 4. since scripture focuses on God's intervention in history and human response, it gives no overall final word on war and peace. The treatment of the Old Testament notes the prominence of the image of God as warrior, explains why such an image arose, and then deals with the gradual transformation of God as warrior into a more complex understanding of God. Treatment of war in the New Testament begins with military images in the New Testament, and moves to focus on Jesus as the announcer of the Reign of God, a realm of justice and peace. This entire section reflects the influence of biblical scholarship.[40] 'Economic Justice for All' similarly surveys the biblical witness on the role of material resources and work among the people of God.[41] The Canadian bishops' 'New Hope in Christ: A Pastoral Message on Sickness and Healing' surveys Old and New Testaments on healing;[42] 'Ethical Relections on the Economic Crisis' selects as normative two biblical themes: the role of work in God's creation, and the preferential option for the poor.[43]

The USCC's 'Partners in the Mystery of Redemption', the pastoral on women,[44] though more recent, lacks a Bible survey. We hope this indicates episcopal comprehension of the dismaying spectrum of biblical treatment of women; nevertheless, it is appalling that they forego this opportunity to instruct the laity in the complexity of discriminating the revelatory from the counter-revelatory messages on women in the Bible, or even to acknowledge that counter-liberatory messages abound. Instead of recognizing the Bible as one of the traditional supports for injustice against women in church and world, the bishops continue papal tradition of selecting positive biblical passages on women,[45] such as examples of Jesus' respect for women and Genesis on the creation of male and female in the image of God. Reference to liberatory passages without mention of problematic/counter-liberatory ones reinforces lay attitudes towards the entire Bible as revelatory, and fails to empower women to resist counter-liberatory messages in the Bible.

In one of the few biblical references in 'Partners' the bishops state that Pauline theology in Ephesians 5.22–32 and Colossians 3.18–21 is important for understanding the Christian vision of marriage and family life, 'even though some of the details found in these passages are conditioned by the cultural patterns of the New Testament era. Their fundamental emphasis is the Pauline teaching that disciples of the Lord should experience a mutual charity rooted in Christ.'[46] It seems unconscionable to interpret the inequality and subjection of women, and the near idolatry of men in Eph. 5, as a 'detail' conditioned by first-century life: 'Wives, be subject to your husband as to the Lord. For the husband is the head of the wife, as Christ is the head of the Church . . .' (Eph. 5.22–23). This is the passage from which we should take '*mutual* charity'? Since Vatican II, especially in John Paul II's teaching, the centre of church teaching has been the dignity and personhood of all humans as created in the image of

God and redeemed by Jesus Christ. This dignity is the basis for the demand for justice. How can the demand that women be subject to husbands as to the Lord – as if their husbands had called them into being and given them their nature and purpose – not conflict with the oft-cited gift of dominion over the earth and its creatures given by God to both men and women? How can the bishops ignore the fact that this passage continues: 'Slave, be obedient to those who are your earthly masters, with fear and trembling, as to Christ' (Eph. 6.5)? The historical conditioning seems obvious in more than details; the mutual charity is extremely obscure.

Also in 'Partners', the bishops write:

> The use of the marriage covenant to symbolize the church's relationship to Christ is prefigured in the Old Testament description of Israel as the bride of Yahweh. Israel's relationship to God is described as a drama of mutual love and fidelity.[47]

This representation ignores the dominant biblical use of 'harlot' and 'whore' for Israel to describe her faithlessness – which established a model of the submissive, feminized covenant partner as morally weak and sometimes requiring the use of threat and force against her by the dominant groom. The bride/groom analogy for Yahweh/Israel and later for Christ/church may well have developed from an attempt to endow these relationships with the intimacy associated with marriage, but it has functioned to legitimate a marriage model in which, because men represent divinity, women are their creatures, however well cared for and loved.

Sometimes the bishops' Bible quotations are appallingly careless, as in the 1979 US pastoral letter on racism in which the phrase '[neither] slave nor free' was omitted from their quotation of Gal. 3.28, which *should* read: 'there is neither Jew nor Greek, slave nor free, male nor female, for all are one . . .'[48] A very curious omission!

In the US bishops' 1980 pastoral letter on capital punishment one of few Bible references concerns reasons for opposing capital punishment:

> . . . abolition of the death penalty is more consonant with the example of Jesus, who both taught and practiced the forgiveness of injustice and who came 'to give his life as a ransom for the many' (Mark 10.45)[49]

Nowhere, even where the bishops point out the possibility of executing innocent persons, is there any reference to Jesus as victim of capital punishment, which we do find in the Canadian bishops' document on capital punishment, 'A Spiral of Violence'.[50] This probably results from overemphasis on Jesus' willingness to atone for human sin through his death, which prevents our seeing his death as an unjust event which should not have happened. We ignore the biblical evidence that Jesus fled his enemies, and was often sly and cunning when his enemies tried to trap him into treason and heresy. He pursued not a way to die, but the Kingdom of God.

Conclusion

While both papal and North American episcopal documents are more informed by biblical scholarship than CDF documents, it is distressingly clear that the *magisterium* of the church has hardly begun to fulfil in any direct way its obligation to teach scripture to the faithful. Ideally, such teaching should begin at the parish level through the Sunday sermon. But in the absence of episcopal and papal teaching on how and what of biblical scholarship should be appropriated, even the parish clergy who have been trained in biblical scholarship are hesitant to teach it. Much of the laity might well be initially shocked to learn that the conquest of Canaan was not a sudden military campaign, but a gradual infiltration, that St Paul did not write the Pastoral Epistles, that some of the apostles were identified as zealots, or that no two Gospels tell the same story of the resurrection discovery.

But North American laity exposed to biblical scholarship in fast-growing lay ministry programmes, or in Catholic universities, are increasingly asking: 'Why has biblical scholarship been suppressed in the church? Why were we never taught to read the Bible critically and contextually?' Increasingly, the choice before the *magisterium* is not whether or not to avoid scandal, but which group of the laity will be scandalized.

In Vatican II the church reformed the *practice* of the faith in the light of the modern world. Rather than ignoring biblical scholarship which might provoke challenges to traditional teaching, the magisterium now needs to face the major task remaining from the opening initiated in Vatican II: the theological task of examining church *doctrine* in the light of developments in biblical and theological scholarship, in church practice, and in our modern world.

Notes

1. *Acts Apostolicae Sedis (AAS)* 35, 1943, 297–325.
2. *Catechesi Tradendae*, *Origins* 9:21, 336, no.27, 8 November 1979.
3. 'Revelation and the Work of Biblical Scholars', *Origins* 9:1, 14, 24 May 1979.
4. Ibid., 14.
5. *Catechesi* (n.2), 343f.

6. Address to Cardinals, *Origins* 12:26, 415, 9 December 1982.

7. 'Theology and Magisterium: Self-Appraisals', *Readings in Moral Theology 6: Dissent in the Church*, ed. Charles E. Curran and Richard A. McCormick, New York 1988.

8. *Origins* 15:7, 105–6, 24 June 1985..

9. 'The Twentieth Anniversary of *Nostra Aetate*', *Origins* 15:25, 411, 5 December 1985; 'Address in Rome's Chief Synagogue', *Origins* 15:45, 731–3, 13 April 1986.

10. *Slavorum apostoli*, *Origins* 15:8, 121, 8 July 1985.

11. 'Justice in the Land', *Origins* 10:39, 617, 12 March 1981.

12. 'Threats to the Church's Unity', *Origins* 12:40, 635, 17 March 1983.

13. *Origins* 14:43, 699–713, 11 April 1985.

14. *Origins* 17:16, 270–2, 1 October 1987.

15. *Origins* 11:15, 225–44, 24 September 1981.

16. *Origins* 10:26, 405–8, 11 December 1980.

17. *Origins* 17:22, 390–2, 12 November 1987.

18. See Mark 10.29–30; Luke 9.59–62; Luke 11. 27–28; Luke 14.26–33; Matt. 10.34–39, among others.

19. *Redemptoris Mater*, *Origins* 16:43, 753, 9 April 1987.

20. 'Instructions on Certain Aspects of the Theology of Liberation x:11', *National Catholic Reporter*, 21 September 1984, 14.

21. *AAS* 69, 1977, 111.

22. *Origins* 15:44, 721, no.55, 17 April 1986.

23. L. Goppelt, *Theology of the New Testament*, Vol. 1, Grand Rapids 1982, 101f.

24. 'Instructions on Christian Freedom and Liberation', *Origins* 15:44, 722, 17 April 1986.

25. See for example Goppelt, *Theology* (n.23), 156–8: E. Schillebeeckx, *Jesus: An Experiment in Christology*, New York and London 1979, 405ff.

26. *Gaudium et Spes*, *AAS* 58, 1966, 1035, no.14.

27. 'Instructions on Certain Aspects of the Theology of Liberation x:14' (n.20), 14.

28. *AAS* 68, 1976, 85.

29. Ibid., 84.

30. *Origins* 16:22, 379, 13 November 1986.

31. *Origins* 18:40, 663, 16 March 1989.

32. Elizabeth A. Johnson, CSJ, 'Jesus Christ in the Universal Catechism', *America* 162.8, 2–7f., 221f., 3 March 1990 and similar brief criticisms in the same issue from William Spohn, the Most Rev. Raymond A. Lucker and Avery Dulles, SJ.

33. Official Copy no.538, 28 May 1985.

34. *Origins*, 8:40, 625–44, 22 March 1979.

35. Official Copy no. 538, 28 May 1985.

36. *Origins* 12:44, 697–728, 14 April 1983.

37. *Origins* 16:3, 33–75, 5 June 1986.

38. Official Copy no.503, 1 September 1983.

39. *Catholic New Times*, Supplement, 1983.

40. *Origins* 12:44, 701–4, 14 April 1983.

41. *Origins* 16:3, 33–75, 5 June 1986.

42. Official Copy no.503 (n.38), 2ff.

43. *Catholic New Times*, Supplement, 1983.

44. *Origins* 17:45, 758–88, 21 April 1988.

45. E.g. *Mulieris Dignitatem*, *Origins* 18:17, 265–73, 6 October 1988.

46. 'Partners', no.86, 768.

47. Ibid., no.87, 768.
48. 'Brothers and Sisters to Us', *Origins* 9:24, 383, 29 November 1979.
49. 'Statement on Capital Punishment', *Origins* 10:24, 376, 27 November 1980.
50. Official Copy no. 546, 25 March 1986, 2.

Uses and Abuses of the Bible in the Liturgy and Preaching

Sean McEvenue

Introduction

The word 'hermeneutics' means simply 'theory of interpretation'. It can make us nervous because it is radical, and it suggests that maybe we have never quite known what we are talking about. Still we need to think about interpretation both in the Catholic churches and in the Protestant churches.

In the Protestant churches the problem is due mostly to scholarship. Over the last two hundred years, the brilliant contribution of scholarship toward an accurate understanding of the Bible has made biblical texts ever more meaningful to the ancient contexts in which they were written, but ever less applicable to our contemporary spiritual needs. Suddenly the Bible can seem a burden, a wearisome set of problems and uncertainties, rather than a liberating Word of God.

Even the scholars are not happy. Several Protestant scripture scholars have told me that, for example, they experience the scholarly 'documentary hypothesis' concerning the Pentateuch as an oppressive constriction. They are delighted with recent methods of reading scripture which enable them to break free from those bonds! For others, the ancient meaning of biblical texts represents a conservative authority, an oppressive denial of contemporary knowledge, to the point where they are obliged to read the Bible one way in the university and in an entirely different way in the church. This is deadly for those for whom the Bible is the only Word of God.

In the Roman church, the problem arises in connection with the liturgy. The Second Vatican Council decided that the liturgy should be in the vernacular, and that meant that the ritual words changed their function from being a sacred sound to being a communication of meaning.

Moreover, the Council introduced the practice of reading a considerable quantity of biblical texts in the liturgy, texts with which many Catholics had not been very familiar. Since that time, the liturgy, for many, ceased being a prayerful encounter with God, and became rather a failed communication and an aesthetic disappointment.

This problem is crucial. Human beings need liturgy, as much as they need friendship. If the church does not provide a satisfactory symbolic enactment of our union with God, then people will go elsewhere for it!

Liturgy is essentially an aesthetic act, composed of literary texts, musical compositions, and dramatic activities. In the Roman Mass, we are taught that Christ is truly present in the appearances of bread and wine, and is not present if the bread and wine do not appear to be bread and wine. If the symbol of the Last Supper and of the death of Christ is not artistically present there, if the aesthetic act does not succeed, then the Mass is not valid. Since the Second Vatican Council, the task is more demanding, because now this symbol must be framed within a context of meanings expressed in prayers said in our own language, in readings of scripture texts, and in a homily. Neither the average parish priest, nor the average Catholic parishioner, is certain about how spiritual truth can be drawn from ancient texts. The readings and the homily often do not provide us with a spiritual meaning. In fact, they sometimes depress us and close off our minds and hearts. Thus the symbol enacting our union with God is threatened, if not destroyed. The experience of these problems has driven scholars to create a jungle of hermeneutics, in an intense desire to clarify issues of meaning and interpretation, so that Protestants and Catholics may once again find the Bible to be, not a burden, but rather a liberation, a release into the sunlight.

One important step toward a solution will consist in understanding the nature of literature, and the relation between literature and truth, literature and moral judgment, literature and spirituality. The Bible consists of literary texts, written in various literary genres. The Bible does not contain theological texts. The Bible is not written as scientific statement, as factual history, as philosophical thesis, or as logical controversy. All of these are literary conventions unknown to ancient writers. No text of the Bible is written that way. Everybody knows this. But our uncertainty about literature, about the seriousness of literature, and about moving from a literary text to encounter with ultimate Reality, along with our failure to deal with these uncertainties, may have led us, both Catholics and Protestants, into the problems outlined above.[1]

It will be helpful to move to a concrete example, despite the limitations of any example, rather than continue with abstractions and generalities.

An example

Last December 31 I happened to go to Sunday Mass at a parish in New Orleans. It was the Feast of the Holy Family, and the liturgy called for reading the following texts: Sirach 3.2–6, 12–14(17); Colossians 3.12–21; Matthew 2.13–15, 19–23.

The sermon was upbeat. It consisted of two developments. The first argued that, despite daily reports of divorce and child abuse in North American families, one must be encouraged by the evidence of significant moral progress through treating wives as truly equal to their husbands, and through respecting the rights and liberty of children. The second reflected on the idea that, although the scriptures tell us little about the family relations within the Holy Family, still it is evident that each member of that family played an important role in the history of salvation, and each role was diverse from the others and respected by the others. The sermon was, then, a moral exhortation to mutual respect.

Refined as this exhortation was, it must be noted that I can remember no effective invocation of church, or eucharist, or mystery, or Trinity, as the basis for our practice of respect. So the sermon was weak. Moreover, no attempt was made to relate the message to specific texts of the Bible, and certainly not to any of the texts we had just read. As a result, the reading of three scriptural texts was made irrelevant. These were not easy texts. Their reading had set in motion a set of images and a series of questions in my mind, an involvement with the Spirit and a beginning of prayer, which were simply broken off by the sermon. It was as though an orchestra played the overture to a symphony, and suddenly broke off and played a sonata written by another composer. In effect, the rest of the Mass then followed after the sermon as though the scripture had never been read, so great was the *caesura*, the artistic gap introduced between the texts and the sermon.

That admirable New Orleans homilist, whose liturgical style was otherwise prayerful and elegant and graceful, had all but cut off my experience of union with God. Now the fault was not primarily his. It was the liturgical authority which, in assigning readings, led him astray.

If we start with the Sirach text, we have first to notice that the text assigned had excluded verses 7–11. Verses 15–16 were also excluded. Verse 17 was placed in brackets, with the foreseeable effect that the reader did not read verse 17 at all. In fact the leaflet published by the Oregon Catholic Press, and distributed at the door of the church, did not print verse 17. There results a text which begins, 'The Lord sets a father in honour over his children; a mother's authority he confirms over her sons', and which ends, 'For kindness to a father will not be forgotten, it will serve as a sin offering – it will take lasting root.' The reduced text reads easily, and seems to present a very simple idea. In fact, the reader should see for him/herself that it is difficult to move beyond the unidimensional idea that children must honour and obey their father (and also their mother), first because God orders this, and second because God will reward compliance. That is a pretty thin idea! Can one blame the priest for not trying to build a sermon on it? Especially when there were virtually no children present at the Mass!

But how about the omitted verses? This is after all a literary text. And the very first, and only really rigid, rule in literary theory is that texts must be read from beginning to end, as the meaning of each word is not determined by definition (as it is in scientific and theoretic writing) but only by the relations of all elements of the whole text to all others. Of course parts of texts may have some independent integrity, but certainly within any part of a text, you simply denature the meaning when you cut out words and sentences.

Moreover, I would contend that no literary text, and no biblical text, expresses such a linear and unidimensional thought as was suggested above as the meaning of the reduced text. Scientific and theoretical writing may want to define concepts and secure logics in such a way as to achieve a single univocal meaning. But literary writing has an entirely different aim. It aims to communicate the experience of the author to the reader, and to communicate that experience in a unified form which is shaped in such a way that the reader can be expected to reach the pre-conceptual insight which the author has arrived at. Thus for example, a national anthem will evoke images and feelings and ideas and historical moments all at once, so as to convey a unified attitude and understanding about one's country. This attitude and understanding could, perhaps, be broken down into psychological components, factual components, political components which could be expressed conceptually in psychological jargon, historical summary, political theory. But the national anthem does not do this. Rather, it expresses a whole human way of being in the world, a composite of awareness which is wonderfully bound into a single artistic experience, a single pre-conceptual insight.

Now chapter 3 of Sirach is not the most powerful passage in the Bible, but still it is literary in nature, and thus far richer than the reduced text might lead one to perceive. Moreover, like all biblical (literary) texts, it includes a perception of God's presence and activity within its way of being in the world. One has to read it as one reads all literature, i.e. patiently and repeatedly, with a readiness to glimpse a hitherto unknown dimension. A reader has simply not understood a biblical literary text until he or she has come to share the author's experience of God in the world, and to share the artistic insight which unifies it. The prerequisite here is, sometimes the scholarship which is easily found in commentaries, and always a depth of faith which can reach towards the faith of the author.

In this perspective, we should attempt to read Sirach 3.2–16(17). Not that the shortened text contained only a trivial idea, but only that the shortened text easily led to a trivial idea.

Sirach 3.2–16(17)

Verse 17 is properly placed in brackets, for it is the first verse in the unity which follows (verses 17–24). Still, a following text is always linked to what precedes, and in this case verse 17 can even be read as a suggestive conclusion: 'My son, perform your tasks in meekness; then you will be loved by those whom God accepts.' The virtue desired here is 'meekness', and meekness is a natural companion to 'respect', the virtue extolled in verses 2–16. The fruit of meekness will be that you 'will be loved' by those who are 'accepted' by God, i.e. the chosen ones, the elect. This is not in the next life, but rather the elect in this life. The movement of thought here is in the area of a sacred community: meekness enhances one's status in a community of love.

The preceding chapters, i.e. 1–2, consist of an analysis of, and exhortation to, the 'fear of God'. In Sirach 'fear' is a word which denotes the central experience of religion, the experience for which Luther used the word 'faith', the mediaeval theologians use the word 'sanctifying grace', and which the mystics treated dynamically in terms of 'way of union'.

Our text, then, at the beginning of chapter 3, is a first application of this fear of God, relating it to status in the community. It develops the idea of honouring father and mother. Verse 7 will say: 'Whoever fears the Lord will honour his father; he will serve his parents as his masters.' And in the other verses of our text the notion of honouring is progressively related to many other family interactions: obedience, praise, not dishonouring, blessing, respect, helping, not grieving, kindness, not forsaking, not angering, and in verse 17 meekness and love. There is built up an image, not just of one-to-one obedience, but of the complex mutuality of a whole family over generations, and the strength of such assured mutual support. This social structure is presented as the place of grace, the place which God blesses, the place where one's love for God flourishes. The causal links are not simple, such as the idea that obedience causes divine rewards. Rather they are complex and reversible. Verse 6, then, is not a failure of parallel logic, perhaps needing emendation, but rather is an apt crossing of ideas: 'Whoever glorifies his father will have long life; and whoever obeys the Lord will refresh his mother.'

In fact, verse 6 would be an excellent place to begin one's sermon, once one has understood what experience of God Sirach was trying to embody and communicate in this text. On the face of it, the opening clause is patently false: 'whoever glorifies his father will have long life'! And the second clause seems almost offensive, as it might seem to suggest that one should obey God in order to please one's mom. This is the kind of line which, in reading literature, one stumbles over, and then stops to puzzle over. One recognizes that it is a key to opening a door: either this author is a fool, or else I am still reading this text without the correct initial insight. Probably the author is no fool. So when I understand this line, the key will fit, and my eyes will be open.

When one understands that glorifying one's father is understood in Sirach 3.2–16 as an extension of one's love of God or fear of God, and as part of a whole network of family strengths, then one can well understand that glorifying one's father will normally result in long life, and even in eternal life. Similarly obeying God, where the ancient word for 'obey' is the same word as 'hear', is clearly not something one does in order to please one's mother! It is a gift from God. The psychic spin-off, if I may speak in those terms, of 'hearing God' will quite naturally find expression in a positive relationship with one's mother. One feels this is true, and the Bible authorizes one to affirm that it is true.

At that point, one might ask why this is so. This would be a specifically theological question, since classically theology is defined as 'faith in search of understanding'. And the answer can, in fact, be found in theological studies of the act of faith, which analyse its content and its effects. The sermon could go into that kind of material, or it could stop short of theology, and turn to the simple purpose of the text itself, namely to urge the cultivation of family respect and love as experience of union with God.

Thus the sermon which the pastor in New Orleans gave was on the right topic. Unfortunately the shortened and denatured text, which doubtless led him to this topic, did not easily lead him to the reflection demanded by a complete literary text. And, apart from Sirach, there was nothing else to help him find a spiritual dimension, a divine presence, within the ethical discussion of respect between family members. His sermon was stuck at the level of good advice, without finding a way to a level of prayer or theology, and without conscious scriptural reference.

Sirach 3 is pretty blatantly an exhortatory text, leading directly to exhortatory preaching. But, as we have seen, biblical texts are always literary. They always have a fuller dimension, as they present, not a simple message, but an author's experience of God. I would suggest that literature is always serious, and always reveals some depths of experience. That is why it is so surprisingly hard to write literature, as only those who have tried can realize. Literature is not just a clever form. It is always also, at least to some degree, an objectification of the self. And the self is inevitably some kind of message, some kind of demand, upon others. Scriptural literature must not be read for theological doctrines, or for laws of conduct. It must be respected as literature, and read for mystery, for presence of God to the writer, for total way of being in the world.

Matthew 2.13–23

We turn now to the third text assigned for this liturgy. I must first point out that the same liturgical authority denatured (or 'deliteratured') this text as well, by excluding verses in the middle. Whoever made this decision, excluded the reference to the slaughter of the innocents, and doubtless thought thereby to focus better on the theme of the Feast of the Holy Family. There is no need to repeat here the points made above about literary texts, beyond noting that the effort to focus on the Holy Family apparently prevented the New Orleans pastor from finding any meaning in this text which he could use in his sermon! This well-intentioned liturgical authority denatured the text by disguising its literary character, and thereby rendered it relatively useless.

We must first discover God in this text. What experience of God does the text embody? What authorial self-before-God, self-as-experiencing-God, is presented in this text? Only when we have answered this question should we proceed to the writing of a sermon.

It is clear that the text has three parts, each one of which ends with a citation from the Old Testament. First, after recounting the flight to Egypt, verse 15 cites the last half of Hosea 11.1, the whole of which reads: 'When Israel was a child I loved him, and out of Egypt I have called my son.' In the second part, after telling the story of the slaughter of the innocents, Matthew cites Jeremiah 31.15: 'A voice was heard in Ramah, wailing and loud lamentation, Rachel weeping for her children; she refused to be consoled, because they were no more.' And finally, in a third section, after the return to Nazareth, we have a reference to Isaiah 11.1, which plays on words to connect the name Nazareth to Isaiah's prophecy of a saviour to be born in the family of David. Matthew made use of these stories, with whatever degree of factuality they embody, in order to be able to cite the Old Testament texts and refer them to Jesus the infant. Matthew's meditation is about the infant, not as a cute little tyke, not as a helpless and endangered child, but precisely as embodying major themes of the history of Israel.

First, just as Israel became Yahweh's people by being freed from slavery in Egypt (and continued as Yahweh's people by being returned from exile), so Jesus is to be understood as one who had to be exiled to Egypt in order to be freed by his Father. And second, just as Israel's great mystery, and ongoing meditation, was the problem of evil as experienced in disaster at the hands of Assyrians and Babylonians, so this infant's life was to be marked by lamentation. And third (as Micah had foretold that the messiah would be born in Bethlehem and Jesus was born in Bethlehem, so), Isaiah had referred to salvation from Nazareth and Jesus was brought up in Nazareth.

Well, all of that is clever enough, but so what? What spiritual message can I get out of that fancy footwork? Does it strengthen my faith? No wonder the New Orleans pastor skipped this text when he thought of writing a sermon. Even in its longer form, it does not seem to have a message . . . Clearly we have not yet got to God in the text. We are not experiencing what Isaiah experienced when he wrote it, nor are we in possession of the insight he wanted to communicate. We have traced some lines of logic in this text. But what world of meaning, what self-in-God's world is Matthew evoking here?

If we read the text again, looking for the key which gives meaning to it, we can sense that Matthew seems to be dwelling on the presence of God in Israel's history: God who is revealed in the Exodus experience which the Jews recover every year in their Paschal liturgy; God who is revealed in the anguish of the exile, which is the subject of so many of the Old Testament books; God who was gloriously manifest in the magical time of David. All of this rich awareness of God's presence in history is evoked, and is applied to Jesus at his very humble birth. This is a colossal act of faith. One either believes it or one does not. (Or one does not quite admit one way or another . . .) An infant with these dimensions . . . ! My whole sense of wonder, mystery, suffering, terror, hope is to be discovered in this single male baby! 'What is man that thou art so mindful of him, and a son of man that thou dost so care for him!', to paraphrase Psalm 8. This is the experience of Matthew, and his preconceptual insight, which he tries to express in a literary form.

Such a shaped experience, if we share it, makes a lot of diverse demands upon us. In the context of the Feast of the Holy Family, one might be drawn to consider the respect we must have for each child, and for each individual member of the family. Each one, my mother, my father, my sister, my brother, my daughter, my son, each one has been given dimensions of meaning in Christ which makes each life valuable beyond my imagination. What respect should I show! What care could be too much in assuring supportive relations, in reconciling differences, in forgiving failings! And so forth.

Once again we have fallen into line with the sermon given by the pastor in New Orleans. But once again we have got there with spiritual dimensions still attached, and in direct reference to the biblical text. It is only by taking the time, by accepting to reread and reread this text as literature, that we have managed to link the liturgical text both to our concrete life today and to a symbol of our union with God.

Conclusion

The point of all of this is that biblical texts must be read as literature, and the homily must begin as would a good class about a piece of literature, so that the being-with-God expressed by the author is shared in the congregation. Any other way of reading scripture is abusive in itself, and useless to liturgy.

In the Roman church a reform is needed. We must review the lists of texts assigned to the various days, and restore their literary character. It will probably be necessary to reduce the number of texts each day: far better one longer text, or at most two texts which really do speak to each other.

Once one begins to treat the texts as literary texts, then the scholarship of the past two centuries ceases to be a problem. Rather it becomes a precious contribution. If the preacher begins by puzzling over the spiritual world of a given text, certain precise questions will arise. These will be questions for which the homilist will have a personal curiosity. Usually, such questions will be precisely the ones which previous readers and scholars have looked into. At that point, recourse to the excellent commentaries now available will be a delight.

Note

1. There is a wonderful short history of some of this hermeneutical confusion in Edgar V. McKnight, *Post-Modern Use of the Bible, The Emergence of Reader Oriented Criticism*, Nashville 1988, chapter 1. McKnight's phrase is 'making sense of' the biblical text, and what follows in this article is an attempt to define more precisely the kind of 'sense' we can legitimately make of biblical texts. The basic source of this presentation lies in the work of Bernard Lonergan, *Method in Theology*, London 1972, especially chapters 3 and 7. A fuller presentation of the theoretical basis for my position may be found in S. McEvenue, *Interpreting the Pentateuch*, Wilmington 1990.

'Listening to What the Spirit is Saying to the Churches.' Popular Interpretation of the Bible in Brazil

Carlos Mesters

1. A fact which shows the direction

It happened during the first meeting of the Bible course. There were about twenty-five people present. On the wall was the sentence, 'God is love.' The priest asked, 'Who wrote that?' 'I did,' said Maria. 'Why did you write it?' 'I thought the wall looked very empty.' 'Why did you choose that sentence?' 'I thought it was beautiful.' 'Where did you find it?' 'I made it up myself. I thought that's the way we have to live as Christians!'

Then the priest said, 'Let's open our Bibles at the First Letter of St John, chapter 4, verse 8.' It took a little while for everyone to find the text. He asked Maria to read the verse. She said, 'Whoever fails to love does not know God, because *God is love*.' It was the first time in her life that Maria had opened the Bible. She got a shock. She didn't expect to find inside it the sentence she had written on the wall. She discovered that, without her knowing it, the word of God was already present in her life. She was so delighted and happy that she hardly slept that night. The next day her Bible was full of scraps of paper marking pages. During the night she had found other familiar phrases.

There are many other simple, ordinary facts like this. They point to the direction of popular interpretation: the gradual discovery that the word of God is not only in the Bible, but is also and primarily present in the lives of *all* those who are trying to live faithfully. The Bible awakens people, reveals and confirms to them that our God is God-with-us, today, here, on the onward march and in the struggle of the poor. The Bible is the source of new attitudes.

In this article the expression 'popular interpretation' refers only to the way the Bible is read by the poor in their ecclesial base communities. There are other ways of reading the Bible among the people; for example, that of the poor in the Pentecostal movements. I shall talk only about what I have got to know and see at first hand. Nevertheless, my horizon is limited. I am only aware of what is happening in some Brazilian communities.

2. Some details of the history of popular interpretation

Popular interpretation didn't come from nowhere. Its roots are lost in the past. In the course of the years three aspects have come to stand out, one after the other.

1. Getting to know the Bible

The desire to get to know the Bible prompted many people to read it more frequently. Let us recall some facts which set this process in motion: 1. The renewal of exegesis, which began in Europe, created a new interest in the text and its content. 2. The three encyclicals on the Bible encouraged Catholic exegetes to be more open and use the sciences to discover the historico-literal meaning. 3. The wide dissemination of the conclusions of exegesis and the use of the missal in the vernacular brought the Bible closer to the people.

In Brazil this movement of renewal was limited to the middle classes. What helped to bring the Bible to the poorest was the missionary energy of the Protestant churches. Many Catholics started to read the Bible in order to be able to answer the Protestants and so overcome their inferiority complex. Gradually, especially after the Great War, this closed and polemical mentality relaxed and the way was open for the discovery of the novelty of the word of God.

In the course of these years, slowly, from within this renewed interest in the Bible, there grew up a new concept of *revelation* which is of great importance for an understanding of popular interpretation. In this God did not only speak in the past; he continues to speak today!

2. Creating community

Just as the word of God began to become familiar, it began to produce its fruits. The first fruit was to bring people together and create community. These are some of the facts which contributed to the people's taking this new step in reading the Bible. 1. People's Bible Weeks throughout the country spread the knowledge accumulated by the exegetes. 2. The distribution of the Bible in the language of the people: in Brazil alone there are more than ten different translations, and more than a million Bibles are printed each year. 3. Scarcity of clergy led some bishops to entrust the administration of parishes to nuns, which, in practice, placed greater stress on the celebration of the Word. 4. In the liturgical renewal and in the celebrations of the Word, the people gradually rediscovered a favourable environment for reading and interpreting the Bible. 5. Millions of Brazilians, relying on the Bible, found the courage to break with the almost absolute authority of the clergy. They abandoned the Catholic church and joined Pentecostal communities. 6. In reaction to the rapid growth of the Pentecostal groups, in some places catechists were trained to go around the villages and gather people together for biblical catechesis.

In the course of these years, from this community ferment, there gradually grew up a new concept of *interpretation* which helped people to understand popular interpretation better. Interpreting the Bible ceased to be thought of as the transmission of information exclusively by the exegete who has studied for the purpose, but a community activity to which all should contribute, each in his or her own way, including the exegete.

3. Serving the people

1968 was the year of the world revolution of youth, the military coup in Brazil, the meeting of the Latin American bishops' conference at Medellín, and the systematization of the theology of liberation. It was also the time when this new step in popular interpretation became more clearly visible.

The community born of the word of God is meant to be a source of blessing for *all* peoples (cf. Gen. 12.3). Faithfulness to the word calls on us to take a step beyond knowledge and community concerns, towards the people. It is here, in the service of the people, that the difference and the novelty of popular interpretation begins to become visible.

The following are some of the historical factors which led the people to take this qualitative step forward in the way they read the Bible. 1. The abandonment of the poor, condemned by the social and cultural system to the status of 'ignorant' and 'inferior'. No one took them seriously or knew them by name. In the community, however, they received names and a history. 2. The military coups of 1964 and 1968 subjected the people to repression, led to persecution of leaders and exposed the failure of left-wing 'vanguardism'. Many leaders disappeared among the people and began more consistent base-level work. 3. After some initial hesitations, the official church became a source of criticism of the military regime. It welcomed and gave shelter to the popular movement, which in this way acquired a strong religious motivation. 4. The see-judge-act method, used especially by Catholic Action, explained and disseminated the new vision of revelation, namely: God is speaking today. 5. The Second Vatican Council and the bishops' conference assemblies of Medellín and Puebla. The Medellín conference was a reinterpretation of Vatican II for Latin

America based on a critical view of the economic, social, political and religious situation. 6. The history of Latin America itself: with tacit cover from the church, Christians killed millions of Indians and blacks and destroyed native cultures. The captivity of the blacks and Indians was worse than the captivity in Babylon. 7. The new instruments of pastoral action in the service of the poor were inherently ecumenical: CIMI (defending Indians), the Pastoral Land Commission (defending land) and the Workers' Pastoral Commission (defending the rights of workers).

All these factors influenced and still influence the way the poor read the Bible. There are communities which, motivated by reading the Bible, place themselves at the service of the people and enter the struggle for justice. Other communities emerge directly out the struggle and, as a result of that struggle, begin to read the Bible.

Without money or ability to read books *about* the Bible, the poor read the Bible by the only criterion they possess, their faith lived in community and their lives of suffering as an oppressed people. Reading the Bible in this way, the poor discover within it the obvious truth which they did not know or which was hidden from them for centuries, namely: 1. a history of oppression like their own today, with the same conflicts; and 2. a liberation struggle for the same values which they pursue today here in Brazil: land, justice, sharing, fraternity, a decent life.

The Bible comes to be seen as the mirror or 'symbol' of what they live today. It is at that point, from this new connection between the Bible and life, that the poor make the discovery, the greatest of all discoveries: 'If God was with that people then, in the past, then he is also with us in this struggle we are waging to free ourselves. He hears our cries.' It is the discovery of God-with-us, the heart of scripture. This is the seed of the theology of liberation. The Bible is the source of a liberated mind.

In the course of these years, out of this attempt to serve the people, there emerged a new way of looking at the Bible and its interpretation, namely: the Bible is no longer a strange book, but *our book*, 'described in writing to be a lesson for us' (I Cor. 10.11), the mirror of our history, or 'symbol', as the Fathers said. The aim of interpretation is no longer to interpret the Bible, but to interpret life with the help of the Bible.

To conclude. What before was distant has now come near. What before was mysterious and inaccessible has now become human and begun to become part of the everyday texture of the life of the poor. And not only that: along with the word of God, God himself has drawn near. This is the Good News which the poor are taking it on themselves to spread across the country. If anyone thirty years ago had made a prophecy and given an exact description of all that is happening here among the poor in connection with the reading of the Bible, no one would have believed them. 'This is Yahweh's doing, and we marvel at it' (Ps. 118.23).

3. The internal dynamic of the process of popular interpretation

In the rural areas of the state of Minas Gerais there is an evangelization movement. Its initial concern was to initiate a process of participation and transmit to the people the new knowledge about the Bible and faith. The political dimension of the service of the people was almost absent. When they were criticized because of this, the leaders of the movement said, 'If the word of God has a political dimension, it will appear in the people's action. What we're interested in is fidelity to the Word.' And in fact the political dimension has appeared with great strength in recent years, and the apologetic concern has disappeared. Today the movement has between 5000 and 6000 groups.

The fact shows that there is an internal dynamic in the process of popular interpretation. *Getting to know the Bible* leads to *living together as a community*. Living as a community leads to *service of the people*. This *service* in turn leads to a deeper knowledge, and so on. It is an endless dynamic. It constantly starts again from the beginning, and becomes ever deeper.

It is not that important which of the three aspects is the starting-point of the process of interpretation. This depends on the situation, the history, the culture and the interests of the community or group. What is important is to understand that any single aspect is incomplete without the other two.

1. Getting to know the Bible. The way the people read the Bible never remains abstract study. They immediately create a community environment of song and prayer in which the Spirit acts. After a careful reading, 'the veil is taken away' (cf. II Cor. 3.12–17), and they discover the connection between the text and the present situation.

2. Creating community. The community rises from the Word like a river from its source. Because of this it always returns to listen to and meditate anew on the Word which brought it into being. It is fidelity to that Word which leads the community to go beyond its own boundaries and defend the lives of the people.

3. The service of the people. In the last few years the communities have embarked on the service of the people. They have thrown themselves fully into the popular movement and have not been afraid to make party political options in the name of their commitment to the gospel. Now, however, this very political activity is calling for a deeper knowledge of the biblical text and a more intense living out in community of the spirituality of liberation.

Generally, in all communities, some people identify more with one of the three aspects and others with one of the others. This produces healthy tensions. If there is an atmosphere of dialogue, a balance is created which encourages and enriches the interpretation of the Bible and prevents it from becoming one-sided. The three aspects are connected with each other in a dynamic unity: one grows out of an other, depends on the other and leads to the third.

At the same time, each of the three is exposed to the temptation and risk of closing in on itself and excluding the other two. In other words, all is not always harmony. Very often the process of popular interpretation is tense and full of conflict. There is always a risk of narrowness and regression.

4. The danger of narrowing and regression

When a community reaches its goal in one of these three aspects (knowledge, community and service), some members, from fidelity to the Word, want to move forward, to take another step. Others, in the name of the same fidelity, oppose this opening. It is a moment of crisis and also a moment of grace. It is not always the group which wants to advance that wins.

In the church all religious movements use the Bible, even the most conservative. Usually all that they do is motivated by the Bible. The fundamentalist movements, in the name of the Bible, oppose interpretation and openness to society. In some places Bible groups which have closed in on themselves and on the Bible have become the most conservative groups in the parish. The poorest of the poor are not in the ecclesial base communities, but in the Pentecostal movements, the great majority of which, for the time being, follow a fundamentalist line.

It is not enough to spread the Bible among the people and think that the word of God on its own will do the rest. Read in isolation, out of the context of the community's faith and service of the people, the Bible is ambivalent and can be manipulated fairly easily. It can become a reactionary book which ends up giving legitimacy to false idols, oppressive ideologies and wars: the extermination of the Indians in Latin America, the slave trade with Africa, the Vietnam war, etc.

There can be a closing in on the opposite side, too, though it is much less frequent. As the community grows and achieves a clearer political understanding and a deeper commitment to service, it may shut itself up in service to the people, in the social and political dimension, and think that the communal and the personal, study, prayer and mysticism, no longer have anything to contribute to the onward journey. There can be absorption in the communal, in mysticism, in the charismatic movement. There can also be absorption in liberal, or even progressive study of the ancient text. These sorts of absorption are tragic, because none of the three aspects alone reaches the full meaning of scripture.

Even in the interpreter's personal life there can be these risks of absorption and regression. What is important in overcoming these temptations inherent in the process of popular interpretation is to be able to create and maintain an atmosphere of dialogue in the community, in which the human word has freedom of movement, without censorship. Where the human word has freedom of movement, the word of God is fruitful and creates freedom.

Despite these dangers, the facts show that the people are able to find the knack of mixing the Bible with life and removing its ambivalence. In a very poor community in a remote rural area of the state of Espírito Santo, the people read the text which forbids the eating of pork and concluded: 'Through this ban God is trying to teach us today that we should eat pork.' These were the arguments:

> God's concern is the people's life and health. In the Old Testament, in that desert, eating pork was dangerous. The lack of water caused disease and damaged people's health. So God ordered a ban on pork. But today we know how to treat this meat. Besides, all we have to feed our children with are these pigs. If we didn't use them, we'd be damaging their health. That's why, today, God is telling us to eat pork.

Why do some communities achieve this openness and others not? The following fact may help with the reply. In the first stage of a Bible course in the same state of Espírito Santo, almost all the questions were about disputed biblical questions: Adam and Eve, the Garden of Eden, the beast of Revelation, the flood, and so on. During that year the diocese came to give more attention to very specific problems of the people: housing, land, health. This had an effect on the second stage of the course, a year later. Those disputed questions no longer held the same interest. Other questions came up, this time connected with the reality of the people's life, both in the Bible and today.

5. The method of popular interpretation

The method one adopts in reading and interpreting the Bible is much more than a set of techniques and dynamics. It expresses, actualizes and transmits a particular vision of the Bible and revelation. That is why not just any method will do. The three aspects we looked at earlier are also characteristics of the method used by the poor in reading the Bible. They are like the three apexes of a triangle.

1. Serving the poor – starting from real life. The poor bring their real-life problems with them into the Bible. They read the Bible in terms of their lives. They have in their minds the situation of the people they want to serve. In the *mirror* of the Bible they meet the reflection of their own lives. The produces in them a certain *familiarity* with the Bible.

2. Creating community – starting from the community's faith. The poor read the Bible with eyes filled with the faith of the community which tells them, 'The Bible is God's word. Jesus is alive and present among us.' Reading becomes a community activity, a prayerful activity, an act of faith. The poor recreate, without a label and without the name, in a new and updated form, the centuries-old practice of the *lectio divina*. The Bible is seen as the community's book, *our* book, things 'described in writing to be a lesson for us' (I Cor. 10.11). This creates a certain *freedom* in them.

3. Getting to know the Bible – respecting the text. The poor read obediently, that is, they have a deep respect for the text. Sometimes this obedience resembles fundamentalism. They are straightforward people, without much critical sense, and open themselves to listen to what God has to say, ready to change their lives and fight, if he demands it. What comes

Freedom

Spirit = Prayer

Creating community = Faith

LISTENING
TO GOD
TODAY

Real life

Serving the people

Familiarity

Studying the text

Getting to know the Bible

Fidelity

through here is an attitude of *fidelity* on the part of people who not only hear the Word, but also seek to put it into practice.

The triangle diagram helps to illustrate what we have just discussed. Each of the three apexes has its own characteristics and requirements in the process of interpretation. When the Bible is read, the three interact to contribute to the common objective, *listening to God today*.

United and acting in conjunction, the three criteria constitute what might be called the spirituality of popular interpretation, its trademark. The three are always present, in one way of another, when the poor read the Bible. If one of them is forgotten, some person or a group will always point this out.

6. The novelty and scope of popular interpretation

The interpretation the poor make of the Bible contains a novelty of great significance for the life of the churches. It is a gift of God, a breath of the Spirit. It is an ancient novelty from the distant past which revives some basic elements of tradition.

1. The purpose of interpretation is no longer to seek information about the past, but to illuminate the present with the light of God-with-us. It is to interpret life with the help of the Bible.

2. The leader of the interpretation is no longer the exegete. Interpretation is a community activity in which all take part, including the exegete, who has a special role. Because of this it is important to keep in mind the faith of the community and look for a *common meaning* accepted by the community.

3. The social position from which interpretation is carried out is that of the poor and marginalized. This changes the approach. Very often, for want of a more critical social awareness, the interpreter falls victim to ideological prejudices and unknowingly uses the Bible to legitimize an anti-human system of oppression.

4. A reading which connects the Bible with life is necessarily ecumenical and liberating. To call a reading ecumenical does not mean that Protestants and Catholics discuss their differences in order to reach a common conclusion. This may be a result. The most ecumenical thing we have is the life God has given us. This life is being threatened, destroyed. An ecumenical reading means interpreting the Bible to defend life and not to defend our religious institutions and denominations. In the present situation of the Latin American people a reading which defends life has to promote liberation.

5. This illustrates the difference from European exegesis. The greatest

problem for us in Latin America is not that faith is endangered because of secularization, but that life is in danger of being destroyed and dehumanized. What is worse is that the Bible is in danger of being used to legitimize this situation with the name of God. Just as in the time of the kings of Judah and Israel, tradition is being used to legitimize idols. Popular interpretation identifies, exposes and denounces this manipulation.

6. The connection between the Old and New Testaments is beginning to be seen with different eyes. Our people's cultures are *our* Old Testament. They have to be seen, not as aberrations to be corrected by the message of the New Testament, but as *our* promises and *our* law to be put into effect and fulfilled by the Good News of Jesus.

7. The method and the dynamic used by the poor in their meetings are very simple. They do not generally use rational, discursive language, built up out of arguments and reasoning. They prefer to tell stories and use similes. It is a language which works through associations of ideas, the primary concern of which is not to *produce knowledge* but to *produce discoveries*.

7. Problems, difficulties and challenges

Not everything is positive. There are many problems and weaknesses. Some have no solution; others are already being solved. There are problems in each of the three angles of the triangle. Let us look at some of them.

1. Life and people
1. Hunger and destitution. It is difficult to talk about the Bible to someone who is hungry and lacks the bare necessities of a human life.

2. Lack of time. Work and the difficulties of life prevent people from taking part in Bible groups.

3. Lack of money. A Bible is expensive, and many people cannot afford one.

4. Illiteracy. Will we be able to create a 'Bible of the poor'?

5. The people's silence. Having been silenced for centuries, they have an inferiority complex.

6. Town and country. The Bible emerged from a rural culture; what relevance does it have to today's big urban conglomerations?

7. People and exegesis. Both have their problems: how can we create an exegesis which helps to solve the people's problems?

2. Community and faith

1. Authoritarian leaders who refuse to dialogue: they oppress others while talking about liberation.

2. The departure of millions for Pentecostal groups produces an apologetic and polemical attitude; where are our communities failing?

3. Lack of training for priests to help the poor to interpret the Bible; the demand is greater than the supply, and the church was not ready to meet so many requests.

4. Conflicting interpretations within the church disorientate the people.

5. In the past the clergy kept control of interpretation; now the *expert* may create a new dependence. How can we respect the faith of the simple?

6. Many people try to tar the liberating dimension of popular interpretation with the brush of Marxist subversion. How can we combine gratuitousness and effectiveness in the struggle for liberation?

7. In the current ecclesiastical climate there is an urgent task to be performed to legitimate popular interpretation in terms of tradition and scholarship.

3. Text and Bible

1. The great variety of translations makes it difficult for people to memorize and ponder on the Word.

2. Fundamentalism is an attitude which interferes with the connection between the Bible and life; liberation from the grip of the letter is the first step towards liberation.

3. The many study guides have the advantage of keeping a group going in difficult times, but may create dependence and kill creativity.

4. In their enthusiasm the people don't pay much attention to the literal meaning; how can we avoid this subjectivism without falling into literalist exegesis?

5. More and more, practice makes one feel the need for a more solid theoretical base.

6. The difficult and strange language keeps the Bible remote from the lives of the people.

7. How are we to reveal to the poor the 'biblical' dimension which has existed in their lives for centuries?

It is very difficult to make a complete and exact survey of all that is happening among the poor in connection with the interpretation of the Bible. The ordinary people don't worry about recording what they do. The poor don't write books, don't cite authors, and don't use bibliographies.

Many of those who participate in this biblical movement are barely able to read. As a result what the people do, when described either by themselves or by someone else, seem not to have much substance. The same is true of this article. It doesn't cite authorities or consult books. The document it consulted is the people themselves, scattered in their communities.

Translated by Francis McDonagh

IV · Conclusion and Synthesis

A Plurality of Readers and a Possibility of a Shared Vision

David Tracy

I. A common confession and historical-critical methods

The emphasis on literary-critical methods of reading the Bible has increased the already acute sense of the variety of possible readings of the Bible in our period. Indeed, as the fruitfulness of various literary-critical approaches to the reading of all texts has increased, the new readings of the Bible *as* literature have also increased greatly. In the meantime, of course, readers of the Bible find a great variety of readings available from earlier and contemporary historical-critical readings of the Bible. In sum, in the modern period, first historical criticism and now literary criticisms have demonstrated the remarkable range of possible readings of the biblical texts.

At the same time, new ecclesial and theological readings of the Bible in different cultural, economic and social settings in our period have also increased greatly; consider the powerful new readings of liberation, political, and feminist theologies alone as new context-dependent readings of the Bible. The central theological question has become how to understand anew, on theological grounds, the unity amidst so wide and potentially rich a diversity of readings.

For this reason, there has been renewed attention in our period to two theological candidates for unity-amidst-diversity: the common Christian confession and the common Christian passion narrative. Is it possible that these two candidates *together* may serve to function to show a pervasive unity of Christian theological understanding of the scriptures without in any way denying the need for great variety? This is the principal theological question provoked by attention to the remarkable new variety of scriptural readings of our period.

To begin with the common Christian confession:[1] the common confession is 'We believe *in* Jesus Christ *with* the apostles'. This means that the religious, revelatory event of Jesus Christ experienced in the present through word and sacrament is the same revelatory event witnessed by the original apostolic communities who wrote the New Testament. It is the revelatory event and not the witnessing texts which must play the central role in Christian self-understanding. And yet the 'book', the scriptures, do play a major theological role. For the scriptures are nothing less than the authoritative witness to that event – a witness to which all later Christian communities hold themselves accountable. To believe *in* Jesus Christ *with* the apostles means, for the Christian, that every present personal and communal Christian belief *in* Jesus Christ is in fundamental continuity with the apostolic witness expressed in the 'apostolic writings' become the Christian New Testament. To believe in Jesus Christ, moreover, is to believe *in* the God of Abraham, Isaac and Jacob and thereby in the revelatory event of Sinai expressed in the Hebrew scriptures and now reinterpreted as the Christian Old Testament in the light of the Christ-event expressed in the apostolic writings.

The complexities intrinsic to any Christian theological interpretation of the scriptures becomes clear. For Christianity is not, strictly speaking, a religion of the book like Islam. And yet 'the book' does play a central role for Christian self-understanding. Christianity, in more explicitly hermeneutical terms, is a religion of a revelatory event to which certain *texts* bear an authoritative witness.

It is difficult to exaggerate the importance of this distinction between event and text for Christian theological self-understanding. To fail to grasp the distinction is to lead into two opposite difficulties. To make the text into the revelation is to turn Christianity into a strict religion of the book on the model of the place of the Qur'an in Islam. Then the route to Christian fundamentalist readings of the scripture under the banner of cries of 'inerrancy' soon takes over. Here Christians believe, in effect, not *with* but *in* the apostles.

The opposite danger is equally devastating for Christian self-understanding: a removal of any authoritative role of the scriptural text in favour of only the contemporary experience of the present Christian community. It is not the case, of course, that such anti-text positions are necessarily post-Christian. The difficulty is, rather, that since the scriptural texts are not allowed to play any authoritative role, the contemporary Christian community can never know whether its present witness to the Christ-event is in continuity with the original apostolic witness. The historical central Christian theological affirmation – 'I believe in Jesus Christ with the apostles' – has been narrowed into the affirmation 'I believe in Jesus Christ'.

Neither of these dangers has been present in the classic interpretations of the role of the Bible in the church. For despite their otherwise important, even radical, differences, all the classic mainline Christian interpreters maintained the hermeneutical distinction between the revelatory event of Jesus Christ and the scriptural texts as witnessing to that event. The text cannot replace the event to which it witnesses. At the same time, the interpretation of the event as present in later Christian communities cannot feel free to ignore its own continuity or lack of continuity to the authoritative witnessing apostolic texts.

It is worth noting that the scriptural texts themselves make the same theological point. These scriptural texts are, after all (as modern historical criticism has made clear), texts of witness by different Christian communities to the event of Jesus Christ. In that precise sense, the scriptures of the New Testament are the church's book.

The New Testament texts, moreover, are, by any reading, remarkably diverse in both form and content. The contrast between the genre of narrative in the Gospels and the genre of letter and exhortations in Paul, the clash in content between Paul and James, the contrast between the tensive quality of the apocalyptic strands of the New Testament and the almost relaxed stability in form of the Pastoral Epistles are differences whose productive possibilities theologians and exegetes are still investigating. What unites these remarkably pluralistic texts is not any single interpretation of the Christ-event (any particular 'christology') but the revelatory and salvific event itself. What unites them is the explicit fact of witness by these early Christian communities to that Christ event. What unites the New Testament, in sum, is the Christian community's faith in Jesus Christ as revelation and salvation. What unites later Christian communities to the early communities is the contemporary community's faith in that same Christ event. What distinguishes the later community's witness from that of these early communities is solely but critically the later community's need to show how its interpretation of that same revelatory event is in continuity to the witness of the original communities. In short, what distinguishes the later community is the presence of the earlier communities' own witness as our scripture.

In this theological content, one cannot but continue to affirm modern historical-critical studies of the scriptural texts. For these studies have clarified the central theological points of the hermeneutical situation itself. These methods have provided historical-critical reconstructions of the original apostolic witness of the different communities (form criticism) and different redactors (redaction criticism). They have clarified both the different social settings (e.g. the brilliant historical and literary analyses of the import of Galilee)[2] and the diverse cultural historical settings of these communities in relationship to their situation. By focussing, for example, on the import of such historical events as the destruction of Jerusalem (70 CE), the Gentile mission, the persecution of the communities, as well as the difficulties occasioned by the event which did not come (the end-times), these historical-critical reconstructions have greatly clarified some of the situational reasons for the pluralism of interpretations of the Christ-event in the New Testament.

That remarkable modern series of historical-critical clarifications of the situational social, economic and cultural pluralism of the early Christian communities has, in its turn, encouraged greater theological attentiveness to our own contemporary situational pluralism. That same historical-theological work has clarified anew the central insight that the scriptures are the church's book: products of and dependent upon the early Christian communities who composed them.

II. The common narrative and literary-critical methods

Moreover, the common confession logically leads to the common passion narrative.[3] Literary criticism has helped us all to see how the Christian confesses not merely through the genre of confession but through affirming the passion narrative as the fuller meaning of that confession. The passion narrative shows us how and why the Christian community 'believes *in* Jesus Christ' – a Jesus we find fully rendered only through the 'realistic', 'history-like' narrative rendering of the passion accounts. That narrative rendering, moreover, Christians also acknowledge as the plain, ecclesial (apostolic) sense of the passion accounts ('we believe *with* the apostles'). The common confession and the common narrative cohere in affirming that plain ecclesial sense (i.e. the obvious, direct meaning of these texts for the Christian community). But only the narrative can show, and not merely state (confess), who this Jesus Christ, present to us in word and sacrament, really is for the Christian community. This emphasis on narrative can also encourage a reappraisal of all the other New Testament genres – doctrine, confession, symbol, letter, commentary, meditative theological thinking (John) or dialectical theological thinking (Paul).

Modern literary-critical and hermeneutical studies have demonstrated the need and fruitfulness of these and other 'genres' for Christian theological use. But all the other genres are helpfully related to both the common confession and the plain-sense of the common passion narrative in order to affirm (or, in principle, to deny, i.e., *Sachkritik*) their Christian appropriateness. This is the substantive discovery of the new emphasis on the common narrative beyond (but in harmony with) the common confession. This position is not narratologically dependent on any particular theory of narrative for human life and thought. It is theologically dependent solely on the plain ecclesial meaning of the passion narrative as that meaning is further clarified by being analysed as a history-like, realistic narrative.

A theologically informed narrative (plain) reading can also clarify how these gospel narratives, as gospel and not merely 'story', are proclamatory narratives of apostolic witness to the proclamation of God's initiative in the event and person of Jesus Christ. Moreover, much could be gained and little lost by showing how these relatively late passion narratives with their 'Jesus Christ kerygma' relate to the earliest apostolic witness of the historically reconstructed 'Jesus-kerygma'.

At the same time, it is the 'plain meaning' of the passion narratives that not merely makes explicit the implicit christology of the Jesus kerygma but also renders in necessary narrative detail how and why the identity and presence of Jesus Christ is experienced as present to the Christian community then and now. If the Christian community means that 'Christ' and the 'Spirit' are present through proclamatory word and manifesting sacrament as well as through various Christian spiritualities of 'presence', then theologically the Christian community should try to clarify how Christ is present as none other than this narratively identified *Jesus* the Christ and the Spirit is present as the Spirit released by Jesus Christ. That identity is rendered through the interactions of character and circumstance in the narrative of the passion-resurrection of this one Jesus who is the Christ of God.

In sum, any Christian theology which confesses its faith in the presence of Jesus Christ (and the Spirit released by Christ) 'with the apostles' will always theologically need the plain ecclesial (apostolic) sense of these narratives to achieve what neither symbol *alone*, nor doctrine *alone*, nor historical-critical reconstruction of the original apostolic witness *alone*, nor conceptual theology *alone*, nor confession *alone*, can achieve: a theological clarification of how the reality of Christ's presence is manifested through the identity of that Jesus rendered in the realistic, history-like narrative of the passion and resurrection: a narrative-confession of this one unsubstitutable Jesus of Nazareth who is the Christ of God.

III. Variety from unity

The centrality of the plain sense of the passion narratives, moreover, should reopen rather than close Christian theological attention to other theological readings. As long as the plain sense of the passion narratives is understood as the fuller rendering of the common Christian confession, then a further diversity of readings of both confession and narrative will inevitably occur.

If one grants the importance of the common confession and the plain sense of the common passion narrative, then a further question occurs. Should the theologian also affirm: first, all the differences in the individual pssion narratives; second, all the differences in all the other parts of the Gospels (the ministry and sayings); third, all the differences in all the other genres of the New Testament?

The different readings begin in the New Testament itself. It is, of course, an exaggeration to say (with Martin Kähler) that the Gospels are passion narratives with extended introductions. The truth in this famous saying is its insistence on the common passion narrative as the heart of the matter. The exaggeration is the seeming downplaying of their differences in the individual Gospels. The differences among the four Gospels are significant enough to demand a theological affirmation of real, i.e., Christian diversity. If one also includes not only the Gospels but also the other parts and genres of the New Testament, then the question of Christian diversity becomes unavoidable.

An opening to the individual Gospels is also an opening to the fuller story of Jesus beyond the passion account alone: his characteristic actions and his typical speech. The different synoptic accounts of Jesus' ministry, his actions and sayings, display to the alert reader how to understand a crucial presupposition of the passion narratives: the importance of the developing relationship through word and action of Jesus to the Reign of God and, thereby, to God. In literary-critical terms, the Gospel accounts of the ministry, moreover, provide the narrative details needed to assure that the relationship of Jesus and the Reign of God are embedded in the Christian consciousness while reading any of the passion narratives.

Consider, for example, the notable differences between Mark's interruptive, indeed apocalyptic, account of Jesus and the Reign of God and Luke's more temporally continuous, even 'history of salvation', account. Since these redactional and theological differences also inform the differences in Mark and Luke in their distinct readings of the passion narrative itself, they call for further close literary-critical and theological readings of the entire Gospels.

Moreover, the same kind of differences have erupted through the centuries in the Christian consciousness in different pieties or spiritualities. It is hardly surprising that Mark's Gospel (so little influential in the early church) now resonates so well with the kind of modern apocalyptic spirituality which informs certain contemporary theological readings of the plain sense of scripture – for example, the Markan 'political theology' of J. B. Metz. It is also not surprising that Matthew's portrait of Jesus as the new Moses and his portrait of the church as the new Israel with a new Torah should have proved so influential in the early church – an emerging community concerned to develop its own institutional, doctrinal and legal forms. Matthew has also proved deeply influential on the community-forming Christian descendants of the Radical Reformation – Mennonites, Amish, Church of the Brethren. Nor is it unusual that the Gospel of Luke (in its full narrative of both the ministry and the passion) allows for quite different Christian readings. Consider the appeals to Luke by charismatic and Pentecostal Christians focussing on the central role of 'Spirit' in Luke. Consider, by way of contrast, how Christians oriented on social justice tend to move instinctively to Luke with his clear 'preference for the poor' (rather than Matthew's 'poor in spirit').

Moreover, the Gospel of John has always been the favourite Gospel of Christian meditative thinkers – whether they be mystics or metaphysical theologians from Origen through Schleiermacher and Rahner. And Paul's renderings of the common gospel in the genre of letter and the conceptual forms appropriate to a profoundly dialectical theology of the cross has rightly been central to many Christians from Luther to Moltmann and Jüngel. Nor do the Pastoral Epistles deserve Käsemann's pejorative dismissal of them as 'Early Catholicism'. Rather, the Pastoral Epistles (as well as aspects of Luke and Matthew) display a clearly Catholic sensibility where doctrine, institution and tradition are prominent. The Book of Revelation, with its wondrous genius at excess, will always appeal to two different kinds of Christians: either those with an historical sense of persecution and present apocalypse; or those apophatic mystics (and, today, post-modern Christians) with natural instincts for excess, intensity and non-closure.

These brief examples of legitimately different Christian readings of the common confession and the common narrative may illustrate that there is no necessity to suspect that either the original Christian communities or the redactors who produced new readings abandoned the 'plain sense' of the passion narratives. But can we really doubt that these different spiritualities, pieties and theologies manifest a finally radical diversity of Christian readings of the common narrative? In sum, the common Christian confession and, more fully, the 'plain sense' of the passion narrative should define but should not confine the possible range of Christian construals of the common narrative and confession. Further attention to the literary aspects of the texts united to the history of their reception, as suggested above, can show these realities of unity and diversity in the detail needed.

The too often underplayed literary aspects of both form criticism and redaction criticism also merit a new look. The productive, not merely taxonomic, nature of the genres analysed by form critics suggest the need for further literary-critical and theological attention to how a particular text is formed through its genre and not merely how a particular historical context may be reconstructed by placing it taxonomically in a genre.[4] In redaction criticism, furthermore, the particularities of the differences also involved in the distinct Gospel accounts of the passion narratives have been further clarified by exegetes like Norman Perrin, who are not reluctant to use modern literary-critical methods of analysis.[5] Recall, for example, Perrin's brilliant contrast of Mark as an 'apocalyptic drama' with Luke and Matthew as distinct 'foundation myths'. These same kinds of redactional skills can allow biblical theologians to attend to the full Gospel narrative of the ministry of Jesus as narrative.

One initial way to assure contemporary theological self-critique in an emerging world church is to take the following step: keep grounded in the common confession and the plain sense of the common narrative, but also move beyond the common passion narrative to the whole of the New Testament Gospels and all other New Testament genres. Attention to the productive character of how genre renders content can help here. The Gospel of Mark, for example, can be read more as a 'modernist' (in literary-critical terms) than as a 'realistic' text. The non-closure of Mark 16.8 reveals the fear, uncertainty and hesitation that Mark's Gospel forces upon the attention of all careful readers – an uncertainty which 'post-modernist' readers do not hesitate to embrace. The uncanny interruptions that disturb the Markan narrative consistently reveal both the apocalyptic sensibility and the strong spirituality of suffering as endurance of radical negativity. The disturbing inability of the Markan disciples to grasp the point of Jesus' words and actions at crucial points in the narrative as well as the pervasive motif of betrayal (Judas) and failure (Peter) should allow any sensitive reader to become hesitant to claim to understand too quickly this disturbing text through purely literary 'realistic' genres.

Or consider a sonic example: the Gospel of John is a narrative that is more like an oratorio.[6] For to read John attentively is more like listening to Handel's Messiah than it is like reading a realistic novel. The rhythmic character of this oratorio-like narrative with its brilliant use of signs and images (light-darkness, truth-falsehood, etc.), with its strange and pervasive irony, and with its meditative, disclosive, and iconic power, releases an attentive reader to meditate even while following the narrative. And was Luther so wrong to sense his own affinity to the genre of dialectic in Paul's theology of the crucified Christ? The tensive Pauline language of 'so much more', 'not yet', 'and yet' released in Paul's relentless and unresolved dialectic is, of course, Jewish. Nevertheless, Paul, through his unique conceptual power, dialectically rendered the searing centrality of

Christ's cross into the Christian consciousness through his rethinking the passion narrative into the genre of dialectical thought.

As theological attention to the narratives and all the other genres of the New Testament expands, moreover, Christian theologians may learn further ways of reading the Hebrew scriptures as now, for the Christian, the Old Testament. Note the illumination cast upon the liberation implications of the passion narrative when those narratives are read alongside the Exodus narrative – as in African–American spirituality and theology, or Latin American theologies of liberation. Or consider how Westermann's Christian theological reading of Genesis can inform the implications of the passion narrative for a new theology of nature. Or observe, with Eliade, how even the cross may be construed, without loss of Christian specificity, as also both the 'cosmic tree' of a cosmic Christianity and the 'tree of knowledge of good and evil' in Genesis. Or note how Paul Ricoeur's sensitive hermeneutical attention to the interplay of the genres of narrative and law, prophecy, wisdom and praise in the Old Testament can clarify, on intertextual grounds, how Christians learn to 'name God' more adequately by attending to the naming of God in the interplay of all the Old Testament genres.[7]

But all these examples serve only to make the central theological point: if diversity is not to become chaos, if unity is not to become mere uniformity, then the dialectic of the common confession and common narrative will always yield new namings of God and ourselves. Literary-critical analysis helps to show this by attention to *form* as often the key to content. Literary-critical readings have thereby joined historical-critical readings to show how the different forms are needed to express in different situations the shared Christian vision of Jesus Christ as the decisive disclosure of both God and humanity.

Notes

1. For further discussion here, see Robert M. Grant with David Tracy, *A Short History of the Interpretation of the Bible*, London and Philadelphia 1984, pp.174–87.

2. See Sean Freyne, *Galilee, Jesus and the Gospels: Literary Approaches and Historical Investigations*, Dublin 1988.

3. For further discussion here, see Hans Frei, *The Eclipse of Biblical Narrative: A Study in Eighteenth and Nineteenth Century Hermeneutics*, New Haven 1974. Id., *The Identity of Jesus Christ: The Hermeneutical Bases of Dogmatic Theology* 1975; and the essays in Frank McConell (ed.), *The Bible and the Narrative Tradition*, Oxford 1986. My own further discussion of the Frei position may be found in 'On Reading the Scriptures Theologically', in the forthcoming (1990) Lindbeck *Festschrift*.

4. On genre study for the Bible, see Mary Gerhart and James G. Williams (eds.), *Genre, Narrativity and Theology*, Semeia 43, Atlanta 1988.

5. Norman Perrin, *The New Testament: An Introduction*, New York 1974.

6. See Amos Wilder, *The Language of the Gospel: Early Christian Rhetoric*, New York and London 1964.

7. Paul Ricoeur, 'Toward a Hermeneutic of the Idea of Revelation', in Lewis L. Mudge (ed.), *Essays on Biblical Interpretation*, Philadelphia 1980.

Contributors

BEN MEYER was born in Chicago and educated in California, Strasbourg, Rome and Göttingen. For over twenty years he has been a member of the department of religious studies, McMaster University, Hamilton, Ontario, Canada. His principal interests, as reflected in his publications, have been in: research into the historical Jesus (*The Aims of Jesus*, London 1979); Christian history (*The Church in Three Tenses*, Garden City 1971; *The Early Christians: Their World Missions and Self-Discovery*, Wilmington 1986); and exegesis and hermeneutics (*Critical Realism and the New Testament*, Allison Park, PA 1989). With E. P. Sanders he edited *Jewish and Christian Self-Definition, Vol.3, Self-Definition in the Greco-Roman World*, London and Philadelphia 1983, and with Sean E. McEvenue, *Lonergan's Hermeneutics*, Washington DC 1989.

ALBERT VAN DER HEIDE was born in 1942. He studied theology and Semitic languages at the Free University of Amsterdam and the Rijksuniversiteit in Leiden. He did his doctoral work on the Targum traditions among the Yemenite Jews (Leiden 1981) and is now a university teacher in the department of Hebrew, Aramaic and Ugaritic languages and cultures at the Rijksuniversiteit in Leiden, where he teaches rabbinic, mediaeval and modern Hebrew. He is also special professor of Jewish studies in the theological faculty of the Free University. He has published studies on mediaeval Jewish exegesis (e.g. in *Amsterdamse Cahiers*, 1982 and 1983; *De middeleeuwse Joodse Bijbelexegese*, Kampen 1985) and writes regularly about the academic study of Judaism.

CHARLES KANNENGIESSER, a member of the Jesuit Order from 1945 to 1990, currently teaches patristics, hermeneutics and christology at the University of Notre Dame, Indiana. He was president of the North American Patristics Society in 1989–90 and is a member of the Institute for Advanced Study at Princeton, New Jersey. Published works include *Foi en la Résurrection – Résurrection de la Foi* (1974), *Holy Scripture and Hellenistic Hermeneutics in Alexandrian Christology: The Arian Crisis* (1982), *Athanase d'Alexandrie Evêque et Ecrivain* (1983), *Le Verbe*

Incarné selon Athanase (1990), and many articles. He also edited
Athanase d'Alexandrie. L'Incarnation du Verbe, Sources chrétiennes 199,
Paris 1973, and is chief editor of several theological series published by
Beauchesne, Paris, in particular *Bible de Tous les Temps*.

GÜNTER STEMBERGER was born in 1940 in Innsbruck and studied
Catholic theology and Judaism; he is now professor of Jewish studies in the
University of Vienna with a focus on rabbinic literature. His publications
include *Geschichte der jüdischen Literatur*, 1977; *Das klassische Juden-
tum*, 1979; *An Introduction to the Talmud and Midrash*, 1982; *Der
Talmud. Einführung-Texte-Erläuterungen* (1982); *Die römische Herr-
schaft im Urteil der Juden*, 1983; *Juden und Christen im heiligen Land.
Palästina unter Konstantin und Theodosius*, 1987; *Midrasch: Vom
Umgang der Rabbinen mit der Bibel*, 1989.

PIM VALKENBERG was born in 1954 in Tilburg. After studying theology
in the faculty of religion of the Rijksuniversiteit and the Catholic
Theological University in Utrecht, he spent some years working in adult
catechesis in the diaconate at Bergen op Zoom. In addition, between 1982
and 1987 he worked on a thesis on the place and function of Holy Scripture
in the theology of St Thomas Aquinas, gaining his doctorate in the
Catholic Theological University in Utrecht in 1990. Since 1987 he has
worked as a university teacher of dogmatic theology in the faculty of
religion of the Catholic University of Nijmegen. His publications include
'Thomas van Aquino als predikant', in *De praktische Thomas*, Hilversum
1987, 11–27; *'Did not our heart burn': Place and Function of Holy
Scripture in the Theology of St Thomas Aquinas*, Utrecht 1990.

CORNELIUS AUGUSTIJN was born in 1928 and has been professor of
church history at the Free University of Amsterdam since 1968. His
publications have been concentrated in the sphere of Reformation history
and the history of Dutch Protestantism in the nineteenth century.

JEAN-ROBERT ARMOGATHE was born in 1947 and has been a priest in
Paris since 1976. He teaches the history of Catholicism in the École
pratique des hautes études at the Sorbonne. His main book is *Paul, ou
l'impossible unité*, Paris 1980; he has edited and made contributions to *Le
Grand Siècle et la Bible*, Paris 1989, and written chapters 15 and 16 of
Storia della Chiesa, 18.2, ed. Luigi Mezzadri, Milan 1990.

CHRISTINE E. GUDORF is Professor of Ethics in the Theology Department of Xavier University, Cincinnati, Ohio, USA. Her PhD is from

Columbia University in joint programme with Union Theological Seminary. She is Roman Catholic, married, the mother of three sons, and has published articles and edited books on feminist ethics, case method in ethics, liberation theology and sexual ethics. Her dissertation was published as *Catholic Social Teaching on Liberation Themes*, Washington, DC 1980.

SEAN MCEVENUE is currently Associate Vice-Rector Academic at Concordia University in Montreal, where he has taught Old Testament Theology since 1972. Formerly a Jesuit, he did his biblical studies at the Pontifical Biblical Institute, and wrote a doctoral dissertation, *The Narrative Style of the Priestly Writer*, under the direction of Norbert Lohfink SJ. More recently his publications have been in the area of hermeneutics, especially S. McEvenue and B. Meyer (eds.), *Lonergan's Hermeneutics, Development and Application*, Washington, DC 1989, and *Interpreting the Pentateuch*, Wilmington 1990.

CARLOS MESTERS was born in Holland in 1931. He came to Brazil in 1949, and there entered the Carmelite Order. He was ordained priest in 1957. After studies in Rome and Jerusalem he was awarded a licentiate in biblical studies by the Pontifical Biblical Commission. He gained a doctorate in theology with a thesis on 'The theme of the exodus in the history of the redaction of the Apocalypse of John'. He was Professor of Holy Scripture at the seminary of the Carmelites and religious in São Paulo and Belo Horizonte from 1963 to 1971. Since 1971 he has been involved in the service of the word for the ecclesial base communities. He helped to establish CEBI (the Ecumenical Centre for Biblical Studies), of which he has been a member since 1978. He has written a number of books and simple articles, including *A Missao do Povo que sofre*, Petrópolis ²1985, and *Defenseless Flower*, New York and London 1989.

DAVID TRACY was born in 1939 in Yonkers, New York. He is a priest of the diocese of Bridgeport, Connecticut, and a doctor of theology of the Gregorian University, Rome. He is the Greeley Distinguished Service Professor of Philosophical Theology at the Divinity School of the University of Chicago. He is the author of *The Achievement of Bernard Lonergan* (1970); *Blessed Rage for Order: New Pluralism in Theology* (1975); *The Analogical Imagination* (1980); and *Plurality and Ambiguity* (1987).

Members of the Advisory Committee for Exegesis and Church History

Directors

Wim Beuken SJ	Nijmegen	The Netherlands
Sean Freyne	Dublin	Ireland

Members

Luis Alonso Schökel SJ	Rome	Italy
John Ashton	Oxford	Great Britain
Hans Barstad	Oslo	Norway
Germain Bienaimé	Tournai	Belgium
Brendan Byrne SJ	Parkville/Vict.	Australia
Antony Campbell SJ	Parkville/Vict.	Australia
J. Cheryl Exum	Chestnut Hill/Ma.	USA
Aelead Cody OSB	St. Meinrad/Ind.	USA
Vicente Collado Bertomeu	Valencia	Spain
José Severino Croatto CM	Buenos Aires	Argentina
Lucas Grollenberg OP	Nijmegen	The Netherlands
Herbert Haag	Lucerne	Switzerland
Bas van Iersel SMM	Nijmegen	The Netherlands
Hans-Winfried Jüngling SJ	Frankfurt/Main	West Germany
Othmar Keel	Freiburg	Switzerland
Hans-Josef Klauck	Würzburg	West Germany
Jonathan Magonet	London	Great Britain
Sean McEvenue	Montreal/Quebec	Canada
Martin McNamara MSC	Blackrock/Co. Dublin	Ireland
Halvor Moxnes	Oslo	Norway
Roland Murphy OCarm	Durham/NC	USA
Robert Murray SJ	London	Great Britain
Magnus Ottosson	Uppsala	Sweden
Elisabeth Pascal-Gerlinger	Strasbourg	France
John Riches	Glasgow	Great Britain
Elisabeth Schüssler Fiorenza	Cambridge/Ma.	USA
Angelo Tosato	Rome	Italy
Marc Vervenne	Louvain	Belgium
Adela Yarbro Collins	Notre Dame/Ind.	USA

Issues of *Concilium* to be published during 1991:

The Bible and its Readers
Edited by Wim Beuken, Sean Freyne and Anton Weiler

This issue begins by looking at the new situation which is arising in Bible study as a result of the development of literary criticism alongside historical criticism when it is again being recognized that scripture can be understood in more than one sense. Later sections look at the way in which the Bible was read in the past by ordinary believers and at understandings of the Bible in different parts of the world today.

1991/1   February   03006 4

The Pastoral Care of the Sick
Edited by Mary Collins and David N. Power

This issue considers the pastoral care of the sick in the light of several years' experience with the revised order of the Roman Catholic church. As well as surveying the content of the revised order and examining patterns of sickness and healing in modern Western society, it looks at healing in early Christianity, the Eastern churches, in Africa, and among women in different cultures, and also at the relationship between professionals and non-professionals.

1991/2   April   03007 2

Growing Old
Edited by Lisa Sowle Cahill and Dietmar Mieth

The successes of modern medicine mean that there are far more old people in the world than ever before, and this number is likely to go on increasing. The existence of so many old people raises important ethical and cultural questions which are discussed here. This issue discusses the phenomenon of aging, presents some theological and anthropological reflections on it, and considers different attitudes to aging in different cultures. In particular it explores how the life of the elderly can be enhanced, and how they can be integrated into society and church.

1991/3   June   03008 0

No Heaven without Earth

Edited by Johann Baptist Metz and Edward Schillebeeckx

This issues focusses on ecology: both natural ecology and social ecology. Against those who say that such problems have nothing to do with the gospel and the kingdom of God it demonstrates that concern with them is what makes the church church. As the church works for justice, peace and the integrity of creation, it is also doing its own special work, for without earth there is no heaven.

1991/4   August   03009 9

Rerum Novarum One Hundred Years After

Edited by Gregory Baum and John Coleman SJ

This issue commemorates the centenary of the encyclical that laid the foundation for the Catholic Church's official social teaching. Articles discuss how this teaching is a response to events already taking place in the wider world; how it is received differently in different parts of the church; and how refusal to apply the best principles of this teaching seriously compromise its credibility in society generally. Main issues focussed on are work, property, the economic situation and the foundation of natural law.

1991/5   October   03010 2

The Special Nature of Women

Edited by Anne Carr and Elisabeth Schüssler Fiorenza

The argument that women are essentially different by nature has been used on the one hand to confirm traditional understandings of their limited place and role in society and church and on the other to argue that they have a unique contribution to make. This issue explores the function of the debate in the church. It contains feminist analyses of how 'women's difference' is constructed, explorations of the way in which it functions in political, social and ecclesial struggles, and the contribution that it makes to theology in terms of christology, Mariology and anthropology.

1991/6   December   03011 0

And for 1992

Towards the African Synod

Edited by G. Alberigo and A. Ngindu Mushete

This special issue has a twofold objective: to allow African churches to speak on the potentially historic occasion of the holding of an African synod, and to make Christians on other continents aware of the significance of an African synod.

1992/1   February   030129

The Debate on Modernism

1992/2   April   030137

Fundamentalism in the World's Religions

1992/3   June   030145

The New Europe: A Challenge to Christians

1992/4   August   030153

God, Where are You? A Cry in the Night

1992/5   October   030161

The Tabu of Democracy within the Church

1992/6   December   03017 X